No Longer Confined

ONE MAN'S TRIUMPHANT PURSUIT OF TRUTH, WHOLENESS, AND FREEDOM

Christopher D. Coleman

iUniverse LLC
Bloomington

NO LONGER CONFINED
ONE MAN'S TRIUMPHANT PURSUIT OF TRUTH, WHOLENESS, AND FREEDOM

iUniverse books may be ordered through booksellers or by contacting:

iUniverse
1663 Liberty Drive
Bloomington, IN 47403
www.iuniverse.com
1-800-Authors (1-800-288-4677)

ISBN: 978-1-4917-2876-5 (sc)
ISBN: 978-1-4917-2877-2 (e)

Library of Congress Control Number: 2014904970

Printed in the United States of America.

iUniverse rev. date: 03/28/2014

DEDICATION

I dedicate this book to my family, friends and loved ones who played a very crucial role in helping me break out of my prison and live an unconfined life. You know who you are. I love you dearly.
    – Christopher

ACKNOWLEDGMENTS

I want to thank all of my personal assistants that have supported me during the writing of this book: Brendan Horgan, Kevin Branch, and Antony Smith. Your patience and commitment to me during this time was immeasurable.

FOREWORD

It is a distinct pleasure to write the foreword to Christopher Coleman's second book. In my life, I have been richly blessed, both professionally and personally, to meet, know and love individuals with diverse social and economic contributions. Sadly many of my friends and colleagues have been reciprocated with exclusion, disengagement and at times hostility simply because of disability, and/or, ethnicity, and/or sexual orientation. What informs a person's faith and practice when their belief is that some individuals are worthy of respect and value and others are not? I will never understand such a worldview.

Life is complex and complicated and we are all vulnerable. Not one of us is immune from loneliness, loss, grief, and rejection. The difference between Christopher and us is that he has taken a risk; a risk that involves great fortitude that few of us have. He has shared his story in hopes of helping others because in fact we are all equal, we are all one, and what he has learned will have relevance for us all.

He writes intimately about love, rejection, friendship, pretension, exclusion, feelings, fears, and concepts of realism and idealism. He writes with charm, humor, and tenderness. He owns his anger, disappointments, and disillusionments, and challenges himself, and by example us, to not become "stuck" in such a harm-filled place.

Christopher has learned the difficult truth that crises must be redefined as opportunities to continue on the path to becoming a better person, and through this process one obtains redemption and growth. Christopher focuses on the challenge rather than the fear of change, which creates a framework for empowerment.

His story teaches us how personal change heightens our self-awareness and compels us toward continual reexamination of our values, our social constructs, and ourselves. This then serves as a blueprint for how to continually strive for a life based on selflessness and service to make one's community, and if we are dreaming big, the world a better place for all.

This book will deepen your appreciation of what is possible, renew your spirit and belief in the human capacity to endure, change and become "better" at being a person who makes a difference, and teach you to celebrate the beauty of diversity.

Nancy Brooks-Lane, M.S., L.M.F.T., L.P.C.
National Consultant,
Disability and Employment

Atlanta, Georgia
March 2014

CONTENTS

PREFACE

As a life coach, motivational speaker, writer and CEO of Unconfined Life Institute, I would like to share my personal story with you. This nonprofit organization is dedicated to initiating and supporting personal, physical, spiritual, professional, and financial breakthroughs.

Because of my profession, it would be difficult for me to just talk about my story and myself. I could not write this entire book without thinking about the individuals who are reading this and how I may help them to pursue an unconfined life. Therefore, at the end of each chapter I have some thoughts and questions for the reader to meditate on while I share my story.

For a long time, I had nothing to go on but hope, and there were times when I wondered if that hope would pull me through to the next day. I didn't know then, as I know now, that I was learning to live an unconfined life throughout my childhood of being confined. Playing the hand that was dealt to me was the key to my freedom. So I did my best and I prayed for the best. Many times I got the worst. However, when it all boils down, I got what I needed through my immediate family, with no thanks to society and the people outside my home.

In this book, you will hear about my family, along with some of the other people who I met along the way. The identities of these individuals will remain unspecified in the interest of legal and confidential issues. When it comes to my family, it is appropriate to say that their story is my story. They too had to face uncertainties and struggles. They too had to persevere through many, many injustices. They had to live with broken promises and broken dreams, just as I did. Many people would label my family as dysfunctional and poor, but they were the glue that held together the broken pieces of my life for so very long.

If I could do one thing while sharing my story, it would be to protect my mother and only to communicate the love and respect I have for her. I know 101 percent that she honestly has done all she could to raise my six siblings and me to the best of her ability. However, like all parents, mistakes were made. Things were said, and situations occurred that were beyond her control. I am aware of some things that must be kept in mind. The first is my mom was raised in a small town sandwiched between New Orleans and Baton Rouge, Louisiana, during the time that segregation was at its pinnacle. I will never know what that was like. Also, she has expressed many times that she did not have the best relationship with her mother. I believe that there is such a thing as a "generational curse," that is, attitudes, perspectives, and sin traits that are carried on from one generation to the next. We are all on some level mimicking the things that we have seen in our own life. I will never know what perspective my mom is coming from. I will never truly understand what it was like to experience racism on that level, being raised in her society, and having to raise seven black kids on my own in the south. What I do know is what it is like to be a disabled black man raised through the early '70s and now living in the twenty-first century. All I can do is share my life story through my eyes as I reflect from my wheelchair.

In writing this book, I wanted to bear witness to what many people did *to* me as well as *for* me in order for me to be who I am today. I also wanted to leave an accurate record of my own life and experience as a disabled black boy growing up and struggling to become an independent young man in the south. Because I believe my story will be important to someone someday, I did my best to be as detailed as possible, while protecting my close friends and loved ones. I would have not accomplished anything in my life without the help of others but, most importantly, without the sovereignty of Christ. Now I know freedom in life and Christ starts with the ability to be who we were created to be. Hiding, denying, or trying to make up for natural God-given weaknesses is living a confined life. Moreover, embracing these weaknesses allows God to prove Himself as sufficient.

INTRODUCTION

"No Longer Confined" is the story of a disabled boy fighting for freedom with himself, with those who are closest to him, with the label he has to live with, and with society in general. I will admit that writing this book was a difficult and challenging exercise. I have never been one to look back at the past. Most of the time, I needed all of my energy to deal with the present.

Putting it all on paper has forced me to deal with old doubts, pain, and regrets. I forced myself to relive the feeling of being locked in a cage and treated like an animal. At times I was shocked at how fresh my childhood experience still felt to me. In fact, it is so fresh that I can only express it in first person. Therefore, "Chris" speaks throughout this book as the voice of my experience.

At birth, the medical team rushed my twin and me to the critical care unit where I was hooked up to oxygen tubes and beeping monitors. Because I went at least fifteen minutes without breathing at birth, I had undoubtedly suffered extensive brain damage. Doctors said that if I survived, I would be crippled and severely retarded. I would also live my life with cerebral palsy, a life between a bed and a wheelchair, as well as a life gripped with seizures.

"He didn't get any oxygen to the cerebrum, the largest portion of the brain. It controls higher mental faculties, sensations, and voluntary muscle activity. Chris will never walk, talk, move, or even think for himself. Mrs. Coleman, I strongly suggest that you put Chris in a home for the mentally retarded and forget he was ever born," the neurologist said.

My mom gave it no thought. She wasn't willing to entertain the idea of dropping me off somewhere and leaving me. A couple of hours later, my father showed up at the hospital. No one knew quite where he was while my mom was in labor. He had a different perspective on my situation. The idea of raising my twin sister, the five kids at home, and myself overwhelmed him. He told my mom he would not be around for all that it would entail in raising seven kids, especially this one with special needs (me); therefore, she may want to reconsider her position. No one could change my mom's mind once she had made it up. She stood firm with the decisions that she made, and no one could deter her. My father's demands were no different. She took me home. He left. From that day on, my father was a stranger that popped in and out of my life.

For the first five to six years of my life, I lay there trapped inside my own body. While lying and sitting there motionless and speechless, I was able to observe and comprehend everything around me. The only thing I could not do mentally was zoom out. I could not take a step back and look at my situation from a larger perspective. I could not visualize the framework that was being built around my life, because I could only see things from my limited perspective. This is where "Christopher" comes on the scene. He is the voice of understanding, my presence, outside of my body. He is able to analyze the things that were really going on and their impact on my life. When my inability to understand the situation occurs, Christopher makes it very clear.

Those who read through my experiences may find themselves anxious to quickly get to Christopher's point of view. Harnessing that anxiety will give great insight into my heart. I too had a constant hunger for understanding in the middle of these experiences. My longing to make sense out of everything facilitated the birth of

Christopher. This anxiety is directly related to the labor pains I had to endure.

I remember feeling like I was born a prisoner. The following thoughts and questions weighed heavily on my mind: *Who am I? What am I?* When they look in my eyes, they say, "*Chris, baby, buddy, little man.*" Whatever they call me, I know I'm not one of them. I don't move like they do. I can't talk like they do. They relate to me differently than they relate to each other. I think they like me. They are smiling at me and talking softly, being sweet and funny. I want them to know I can hear them. I want to smile and talk to them, but I can't. Do they know I understand them? How do I reply? I feel removed from their world. They are free. I am trapped, trapped in a body that will not allow me to move or communicate.

It cannot be denied; my fight for freedom began with imprisonment. For example, some would say I'm not qualified to speak on the things I will address in this book, in spite of my education, in spite of my personal and professional experience, in spite of the fact that I am a human being who is able to communicate and form thoughts and opinions. Many think that my disability diminishes my credentials. I too have the right to freedom of speech in America. I do not feel a need to hide, sugarcoat, or bite my tongue on those things that have played a negative or a positive role in my development.

People can see the obvious when they look at me. They know that I struggle to pronounce my words, feed myself, and dress myself. But what they don't realize is the lifelong challenges and struggles beneath the surface I had to face in order to get to where I am now, as well as the challenges I continue to face. There are just some things that cannot be seen by my physical appearance. There are some struggles and life challenges that many people do not consider when they think about the life of someone with a disability. In the next chapters of this book, I am going to take you on a lifelong journey beneath the surface of an American black man with a disability. I want to give people the opportunity to see life through my body, on the knees I crawl on every day, and in the wheelchair I constantly rely on for mobility. The reality of my situation has forced me to look at the world through a different lens. I now see life beyond my circumstances.

CHAPTER 1

Born a Prisoner

Hold up, before I share my story with you. First you must read the preface and introduction. If you failed to do so you will miss out on a lot of important information. You may even be lost for the first half of my story. So, I am going to play the jeopardy song in my head, while you go back and read the preface and introduction. Okay, are you caught up now? Are we all on the same page?

Those who read my first book, *Solitary Refinement*, often say that I have great insight for someone my age. However, I wouldn't call it insight as much as it is experience. The previous book is a blueprint for a life of freedom. Though it is difficult to relive the past, it is a way to see and track my path to freedom. I am going to roll up my pant legs and let you see the cuts, scars, calluses, and blisters from a journey I first had to crawl. Yes, crawl. Living in this world with a disability means that the individual has to crawl his way through life. It was a rough, hilly, sometimes slippery, and many times muddy path I had to travel in order to get up to the top of the mountain and declare out loud, "I am *no longer confined*!"

There are roughly 650 million people who live with a disability. What are their lives like? Where are they? Who takes care of them? Are they able to live productive lives in the society that they are in? What do they believe about themselves? What do people with disabilities believe about religion and having a connection with God? These questions and my answers have produced many issues, issues that have affected my life in such a way that my worldview has been shaped by them. There have been many pros and cons resulting from these concerns.

Though my life is physically hard, my greatest challenge in life will not be my physical condition; it will be the people around me. They will answer questions for me, they will pretend to know what they don't understand, and they will push me aside and act as if I don't exist. When all else fails, they will use me, all because it makes them comfortable. Many will try to confine me to their beliefs, limited understanding, and comfort zone. Some of them will be family, some doctors, friends, teachers, and preachers who proclaim that God has a plan for everyone's life and everyone is welcome in their churches. In so many words, society will say, "We can't explain it. Therefore, we are uncomfortable with it, so let us come up with some way we can live with it."

The *it* is me.

The Voice of Experience: Chris

I hate having seizures. My whole body starts to hurt. It gets worse and worse. It feels like I'm going to black out and lose control of my body. My mouth gets so tight, and my tongue jumps around in my mouth like crazy. Then it gets hard for me to think and see. I try to fight it and stay awake, but it takes over sooner or later. I ask myself every time, "Why is this happening again?" After that, it gets completely dark, and I can feel my whole body jerking.

I don't know how much time goes by before I hear Paul say, "Momma, Chris is waking up from his seizure." The pain is still there. I still feel so weak and sleepy. A lady appears in the doorframe, holding my four-year-old twin sister. She is called Gladys by some,

Ms. Coleman by others, and Momma by the young people in my life every day. Today, she is wearing her long day outfit. Her hair is rolled up on little black plastic sponge rollers covered by a red scarf. Because of her broad shoulders, her red-and-white T-shirt seems to be hanging off her until it reaches her hips. She likes to be comfortable on these days, so her slightly faded blue jeans fit her looser than most. To top off her outfit and finish the look, she has on her slightly worn down red-and-white Reebok tennis shoes.

I love her so much. I hate the days when she is not here. Even though my brothers are taking good care of me, I miss her presence. Things are not the same when she is gone to work. She has put down my sister to hold and rock me now. She wants me to think that everything is OK, but I can tell she is tired. She doesn't want me to see it, but when she looks down at me, there is a strain behind her smile and in her eyes. "Momma loves you," she says. I don't know why, but when she says that, I feel like I'm free. For a moment, I forget I'm trapped. She gives me a hug, but my inability to hug her in return brings me back to reality.

It is no surprise that Paul is sitting by my bedside. I feel so close to him. He makes sure I have everything I need. He seems to love me just as much as Momma. I can feel his heart for my condition. Lamont, just like Paul, is always here too. There are very few times I have seen one without the other. They look close in age but completely different. Paul has darker skin, is taller, and is slightly heavier than Lamont; while Lamont is more tan, shorter, but just as heavy as Paul. They are my two guardian angels in our home. I can tell that they totally enjoy being around me. I know that if I ever need anything, Paul and Lamont will be there for me.

I can hear Dewayne and Russell arguing and wrestling in the other room. They are the reverse version of Paul and Lamont. Though Dewayne is older, he is smaller than Russell, light skinned, with really curly hair. Russell is taller, dark like my older brother Paul, and has a baldhead. Those two are always up to something. I don't have a strong connection with them yet. However, they are always looking out for me by helping to change, dressing, and feeding me daily. Even though they are not much older than me, they do as much as they can for me.

My big sister Angela and my twin sister Christina are too little to help me. I can tell they don't quite understand why I am the way I am. There are times when they don't seem to like me very much. I get the sense that when Momma is holding me, they feel I am taking something away from them. I can tell by the way they look at me out of the corner of their eyes and the way they pinch me that they are not very happy with me. I guess that's OK, because I am always imagining myself reaching up and grabbing their long pretty black plaits and pulling on them. I think they don't like me because I steal a lot of Momma's time and attention when she is not at work. I'm not sure I feel sorry for that at the moment. I love it when Momma's around.

I believe everyone in the house loves me and cares for me, but I have a different relationship with them than they do with each other. It seems like Paul and Lamont are best friends and do everything together. Dewayne and Russell are always talking about girls, and they have a lot of the same friends in common. Angela and Christina have the common bond of being the girls in the family; therefore, they played together all the time. Then there is me, who for the last four and a half years has been going in and out of seizures, from the hospital to doctors' appointments. I have no common bond with any of them other than the fact we share the same home. I am the misfit.

My older sister and my twin sleep every night on a pullout bed in the living room. Dewayne and Paul sleep in my room with me, while Lamont and Russell sleep in bunk beds in the other room. These two rooms are connected together by another room with only a sink and a commode. On the other side of the kitchen, down the hall, are our washer and dryer, a bathroom, and Momma's room. On the nights when I have seizures, I sleep with Momma. I love it. I have her undivided attention on those nights.

I can tell we all work together to get things done. Our home is always spotless. My siblings, including my six-year-old older sister, have to help keep the house clean. On days they don't clean the house well, it is trouble for everyone. Momma says all the time, "If I'm going to be the one that works all day to put food on the table, then you kids better keep this place clean." My brothers and sisters do a pretty good job at it. But if my mom has a bad day at work and needs to let off some steam, she comes home in her spring-cleaning mode and says the house "looks like dogs live in here." Everyone is miserable on those days. Momma chews out each of my brothers and sisters, one by one, for something they are not doing right. The funny part is even I know better than to ask Momma for something when she is in this mood, but my older sister Angela has not learned this lesson yet. If I could shake my head at her, I would! She should know by now that Momma is not going to like being bothered when she is in this mood.

On the many days when Momma is at work, we go across the street to the fairground. In the back of the grounds is a neighborhood park. All of the kids in the neighborhood spend many after-school evenings and summer days playing here. Everyone loves it except me. I hate it. I'm just sitting here alone under a tree, in the same spot they put me in every time we come here. I feel like our dog, Tiger, chained to a tree. I do not like sitting here watching the kids do the things that I can't do. When I look straight in front of me, I see my sisters swinging back and forth on ropes with cracked old seats that are tied to rusted poles in the ground. They are laughing, giggling, and shouting things back and forth between themselves. Every now and then, Angela will look back at me and shout, "Hey, Chris!" Next to them are kids hanging from a rusted old domelike structure called the jungle gym, which looks like it is going to fall with all the kids on it. Nearby, there are more kids having fun going backward and forward on the monkey bars. On the other side of the swings, the kids are climbing up a ladder on the back of the slide and then sliding down. I can hear the back of their legs scraping the slide as they go down. That must hurt, but it still looks fun to me. All I can do is sit here under my tree and wonder what it must be like.

As I look across the playground, I see Paul, Lamont, Dewayne, and Russell running back and forth with a whole group of other boys. It seems like one team is trying to get the ball into the rusted circle mounted on the pole, while the other team tries to prevent them from doing it. When each of my brothers gets a slow moment in the game, they slightly bend down, rest their arms on their knees, take a deep breath, look over at me, and give me a wink just to let me know they are paying attention and I am OK.

But I'm not OK. I don't like being here. Even though I am far away from them, I can feel the tension as I watch them go back and forth. Paul and Lamont are bumping their bodies against other boys their size. I can tell they are about to get into a fight. They are shouting to Dewayne and Russell to stand back. Fighting is a very common activity in my family, which I hate. My brothers and sisters fight a lot among themselves. And just like this day, I've seen them stick together on the playground against the other kids.

While sitting under the tree, many kids continuously come by to make fun of me. They make faces at me, ask their parents what is wrong with me, or show me to their friends by pointing their fingers at me. Many times, I imagine biting their fingers off. Every now and then, I overhear the other kids reminding the bullies that I am the little brother of Paul, Lamont, Dewayne, or Russell Coleman. Then they turn around and walk away. I think it is safe to say the Coleman's are fighters, and few people dare to take us on.

I want to believe that one day I will be just as active as the rest of my family, but there is something I don't understand. My older sister and brothers are bigger than me. I get that. I can see why they are moving and talking. But my twin sister, the girl that looks my age and my size, is moving and talking as well. She can't move and talk as much as the rest of them, but she is doing a lot more than I can do. Why is that? Is there any hope for me to be able to move and talk like they do? Why me? How did I get to be the one that is sitting here? How do I fit in with this family? And most of all, why do they care about me? It seems like I am nothing more than just a lot of work for them.

The other day was different. My siblings and I didn't go to the park as usual. Instead, Momma got me up early with the rest of the kids. After getting me dressed and feeding me breakfast, we went outside. We waited for a while, and then a big blue-and-white van pulled in the driveway and lowered a lift. Mom placed my stroller on the lift, and up I went. One of the ladies began to lock me in place, while the other one closed the lift and locked the door. I was so scared. I started to think, *is Momma sending me away? Are they tired of me? I remember so many movies we have watched where a van similar to this comes and takes the bad people away. Why wouldn't she send me away? My brothers and sisters drive her up the wall sometimes. I know I've got to be getting on her last nerve. Is that what's happening to me?*

As I looked around, there were many other kids like me in the van. That was my first time seeing someone like me. I thought to myself, *what is wrong with them? What did they do wrong?* We all had car seats and strollers locked into the floor of the blue seats in the van. I wasn't quite sure what was going on. However, there was a really sweet lady going from seat to seat, playing and talking with each one of us. I thought things were going to be OK, but I just didn't know.

The van finally stopped in front of a place I had never been to before with a lot of new faces. The van finally stopped in front of a place I have never been to before with lots of new faces. The lady who got me out of the van called me "cute." That made me feel good. Momma calls me cute all the time. Maybe this person likes me the same way. She took me inside to a big, open room. There were many colors, shapes, pictures, and ABCs on the wall. The floor was covered with soft padding everywhere. Every corner of the room was filled with books and toys and stuffed animals.

Another side of the room had several mats on the floor where the rest of the kids and I can take a nap after eating. During the day, the teacher allowed us to be free on the floor. Some of the kids were able to crawl all around the room and play with toys, while a couple of us could only watch. We could not crawl and get the things we wanted to play with.

I had many visitors. One lady came to stretch me out while another lady just came to talk. I think she was expecting me to respond to her. So I tried with all my might to do so. Even though she answered yes and laughed, I knew she wasn't getting what I was trying to say. She ended up just making me mad, and all I could do at that point was cry. I was ready to go home. I liked that place, but I wanted to leave. I hoped the van would soon bring me back to my brothers and sisters.

The teacher finally put me back into the van. I was so glad that day was over. I couldn't wait to get home and see my family. I did not know I would have to do it all over again the next day. Momma continues to wake me up, get me dressed, feed me, and bring me back outside to wait for the van. Off I go again. I know my family must be getting tired of me. They're sending me away during the day so they can get a break from me. Right now it's just for a few hours, but eventually they will send me away and I will not be allowed to come back. This is what I am afraid of happening.

I want to find a way to be friends with my family. I want them to like me as much as I like them. I have to become more like them. I made up in my mind; I am going to talk to them. So here I am lying in my bed, trying my hardest to pronounce a word. I just want to be able to say "Momma" out loud. I'm hoping if I push all of my energy toward my mouth, a word will come out. I feel like I am getting close. Something is about to come out of my mouth now. Let me keep pushing. I know something is about to happen. Something came out, but I tried too hard. Now my whole body is sliding out of the bed. Oh, no, I am going to hit the floor!

Within seconds of hitting the floor, I feel and hear Lamont's presence over me. I can feel myself going into a seizure now. Lamont is not grabbing a spoon, wrapping it with a towel, and sticking it in my mouth to hold down my tongue, like they always have done. Instead, he is prying open my mouth with his hands and placing his fingers between my teeth to hold down my tongue. I can see the pain on his face as my mouth clenches down on his fingers. But I have no control. I cannot let go for anything. I really want to, but I can't. Lamont and I are both in the emergency room now. His fingers are bleeding, and he needs a shot. I feel so awful. All of this is because of me. How would I ever get my family to like me now?

Your Moment with America's Unconfined Life Coach, Motivational Speaker, Author, and Confidence Builder:

It is a fact we tend to be harder on the people that are closest to us. We all can find something in our families that is dysfunctional. However, inside of every person is something to be appreciated and something to help us grow.

Are you giving your family a fair chance?
Do you realize they could be doing the best they can with what they have?
Are you seeing the best in them, or are you focused on the worst in them?
How can their character flaws help you grow?

CHAPTER 2

Beneath the Surface

The Voice of Experience: Chris

As I'm looking outside of my front door, I see the back wall of my aunt's white and brown stained trailer. Just a few feet from there is a wooden shed. I'm sure someone made it for her. It's just a few old wooden boards nailed together. If I squint real hard, I can see straight through it. A few feet to the left of that is a big oak tree where our dog, Tiger, is chained. Tiger is a mix of german shepherd and pit bull. He is so protective of everyone. We know when people are visiting because Tiger starts to bark and growl real loud. Right next to him is his doghouse. We have to peep out of the window to see him get in it because the minute that my brothers, sisters, or Mom steps out the door, Tiger comes out of his house and stays out of it until they are no longer in sight.

I am not sure where my aunt's backyard ends and our front yard begins. It's all so very close. Just a few more steps from the doghouse and the tree is a small cement patio similar to my aunt's patio in front of her front door and steps. Both of our patios have a walkway leading up to the front of the driveway and into my grandmother's side patio. The two walkways almost form a perfect "v." They used to not even be here. When I got my oversized stroller, they decided to lay the sidewalk to make it easier for them to push me around. I love it when my brothers, sisters, and cousins push me really fast down the walkway on laundry days. In between the two trailers and my grandmother's house are clotheslines going from one side of the property to the other side. When they hang sheets and towels to dry, we run through them. I love the smell of Downy as each towel or sheet hits my face.

The Voice of Understanding: Christopher

Looking back now, I realize growing up in the early 1970s in the small town of Praireville, Louisiana, with a single mother of seven kids and a severe disability made life especially confining for me. Our singlewide, three-bedroom trailer behind our grandmother's house was just a small step up from what was known as trailer park trash in those days. Four poles in each corner supported the elongated, rectangular-shaped, sheet metal box. It didn't seem like a structure someone could run to in need of a shelter from the tornados or hurricanes that often sweep through our small town down in the southern part of the state. My home's internal, wood-stained paneling was barely thick enough for a nail to hold the very few pictures and really cheap art on the wall. Yet, it was strong enough to hold the emotional storms that a family of eight is bound to experience. It wasn't long after my birth that this small, low-economic community was invaded with drugs, alcohol, and crime. This invasion further complicated my family and moral support, education, and special needs.

Now I know a life dictated by statistics, educational guesses, and premature diagnoses is a confined life. PhDs, teachers, therapists, preachers, and doctors built an environment around me in which hope, faith, and dreams could not live. The individuals in my inner circle were going to be the ones that forced me to live out this lifelong sentence or break me out of the prison I was born in. In my life, there are two kinds of people: one accepts and goes with whatever society says is the norm, while the other rebels and becomes a vessel for change. It is going to take a rebellious group to overturn this verdict. On that note, let me give you a second introduction to my family.

Paul, the oldest (also known as "Big Black"), is my father figure, best friend, and hero all rolled into one. He is like all of my family, a star athlete. He is not much of an intellect and hates authority. His mind-set is to help Mom any way he can, as soon and often as possible. Paul and Lamont are really close. They hang by each other's side no matter what the circumstances. Lamont is a very easily influenced, people-pleasing boy. He cannot stand being in trouble or looked down upon by his family and friends. But Paul is very good at getting him to walk on the wild side every now and then.

Dewayne is what my mom would call "hotheaded." He is very headstrong. He is only going to do what he wants to do, when he wants to do it, for whom he wants to do it for, and how he wants to do it. That's that with him. He is not college material but can fix and drive anything that you put in front of him. Russell is definitely the middle child. Not forgotten about, but after three boys older than him, the first girl, and the twins, he didn't get much attention from Mom. His magnetic personality makes it easy for him to be a little con artist. Nothing harmful, he is just someone you have to make sure is being totally truthful before just buying into whatever he is selling that day.

My older sister, Angela, was, for two years, the youngest and only girl in the family. I don't think having a little sister to compete with and a younger brother with special needs will ever go over well with her. Of all the kids, I think she struggles the most with the absenteeism of our father. She wants to be Daddy's princess. Her dream is to be a supermodel.

My twin, Christina, better known as "Dirty Red" or whom I call the "Evil Twin," is my healthy competition. As the two youngest, we compete for the attention of our older brothers, cousins, aunts, and uncles. Her big brown eyes, light skin, and long black hair gives my childlike personality, big heart, and sensitive condition a run for its money. People did not know whom to love on first. Her nickname says it all. It comes from her knack for revenge. She is the type of girl who is very sweet until you do her wrong. Eventually, she will get you back.

All of the kids are, in some way, like our mother. Chris did a wonderful job at explaining her sensitivity and love for my condition. After all these years, now I know Gladys is also a hell-raiser! I've watched her so many times stomp people in the ground that crossed her and then wipe off her shoes as if those people were just a bug that aggravated her. Raised in the 1940s and a single mother of seven, Gladys has been shaped into a woman not to be taken lightly. There is no one she will not take on. Some people earn respect. Some people automatically get respect. Then there are other people like Gladys who demand respect. She runs our home and our lives with a ruthless efficiency. She has a short temper and quick instinct to pick up a shoe, broom, or use her hand to discipline anyone who needs it. The fear her seven kids have of her is not a result of her parenthood. It is the same fear that everyone has toward her once they get to know this straightforward, bold woman. Let me be clear. Momma is an aggressive, feisty, argumentative strategist. She has a sharp, no-nonsense approach to life. It is impossible to mistake her meaning. She is forthright and direct.

Our home was full of '60s furniture. Mom always came home on the weekends with knickknacks and furniture she bought from garage sales. What wasn't good enough for someone else was perfect for us. I loved sitting around on our green vinyl couch. As I rolled my Hot Wheels cars up and down the back of it, I noticed every day that there was one more button missing. Our rooms were just barely big enough to hold our necessary queen-size beds. It was amazing how three or four of us could sleep and dress in one room day in and day out. To many, this structure was the last thing that they would call a home; however, when we were all there and the chaos of the family dynamics started, that cold, raggedy structure became a warm, loving environment we called home.

What about outside my home? It should not come as a surprise when I tell you that church was a part of my upbringing. The black community in the South relied on their spiritual beliefs. My mom was no different. I was taught that a relationship with Christ is the only answer for everyone. But there are some things I don't understand yet, so I wonder, "Is church really a place for someone like me?"

The Voice of Experience: Chris

A couple of days after a seizure, we went to the church I've been going to pretty regularly all my life. However, today was different. At the end of the service, my whole family and I went up to the front of the church. The guy that always speaks laid his hands on me, while everyone else surrounded my family. The speaker started to talk to God about my situation.

I learned a lot through his prayers. I learned that God created me. Now He needed to fix me, heal me, and release me from this bondage. So, just as I thought, something is wrong with me! It isn't OK for me to be the way I am. I've always felt that I was different from everybody else. This proves it. Now everyone is praying that I would be healed. The pastor prayed over my hands and my feet and my head. But I don't get it. If God wanted to change me, why did He create me this way in the first place? What did I do wrong to be the only one in my home created this way? This is too much for me to think about. They know more about God than I do, anyway.

The Voice of Understanding: Christopher

In Mark, Chapter 2, he tells us the story of a paralytic receiving healing. These verses tell us about a group of men trying to get their friend in front of Jesus. However, there is a large crowd that is not allowing them to walk through the front door. Therefore, they harness the man up on the roof, create a large hole, and drop the paralytic before Jesus. My life as a man living with a disability produces a question about this story. Why did they have to bring this man up on the roof and lower him through a hole? The obvious answer would be it was too crowded.

I can't help but ask myself, "Why didn't these people see the importance of getting the paralytic to Jesus? Wouldn't it have made sense for the crowd to part ways and make a pathway to the front of the line where Jesus was? Is it wrong to expect people who believe Jesus is the answer to say, "This is a man that can't get to Jesus on his own. Let's help him get there"? Were they there for their own selfish gain? It seemed like they were more concerned about getting what they wanted from Jesus rather than what someone else may have needed.

This is why I asked, "Is church really a place for someone like me?" People in wheelchairs are asked to sit in the back in order not to disturb the flow of the worship service. Parents who have disabled children are not able to go to church because there is not a place for their child with special needs. I don't believe it should be this way.

Your Moment with America's Unconfined Life Coach, Motivational Speaker, Author, and Confidence Builder:

When people start to feel trapped or confined to a situation, they may only analyze the walls around them and never take into account the foundation that holds up the walls. The key to our freedom could be buried under our foundation.

When it comes to your family, do you feel like you belong?
How has society shaped your life?
If any, what role does religion play in your life?

CHAPTER 3

Memories from a Cage

The Voice of Experience: Chris

I know I am getting better. I am able to stay up longer. It seems that the seizures are not as bad. I understand even more of what is happening on the television and around me. I know my words are coming out as grunts and moans, but I am really trying to tell everyone what I need and want. When I am at school, I can look at my teacher and then move my eyes toward food, a drink, or toys that I want. I shake my head to tell them things I do or do not like. I don't know why they don't realize I am trying to talk to them. They just say, "Yeah, yeah," and rub my head. However, my mom, brothers, and sisters understand me. It makes me so mad when the teachers don't.

It is so hard getting to the restroom on time. Mom thinks I wait too long to get there, and she fusses at me if I do it in my pants. First, I have to slide off the couch onto the floor of the living room. Then I have to crawl my way into the kitchen, around the table, down the hallway. When I get to the door, I have to go past it because it opens the other way. Then I can't reach the knob of the door so I have to put my hands under the door, wrap my fingers around it, and pull out. After crawling in, I have to turn around and grab the bottom of the door again and pull it shut. Once I reach the commode, I have to stand up on my knees and unbutton the button. I hate buttons. Then get the zipper down and pull my pants down. Finally, I have to place both hands on the side of the tub and push up on my hand and legs. When I am high enough, I let my body fall back, hoping not to miss the commode.

After all of that, it still takes too long most of the time. I didn't make it. I tried to go as soon as I felt like I had to. I hate the fact that someone has to change me like I am a little baby. It takes so much time to get my clothes off, put me in the tub, get me out the tub, and rinse off my dirty clothes. I wonder if everyone else feels the need to go sooner than I do. I can't understand why I keep messing my pants. God knows I hate it when this happens.

Today I made it to the bathroom on time; I just had to pee. I thought, because I was here, I would have a little fun. So I decided to open the bottom cabinet under the sink and see what I can play around with. There are several bottles. One says Clorox; and the others say shampoo, conditioner, Windex, and laundry detergent. I decided to play like I am cooking soup. I put a little bit of this and a little bit of that into the commode. Ammonia, let's put that in too. I used the commode brush as my spoon; round and round everything went. For a while, I just stirred up everything real good. Then I decided to leave before my momma would catch me, or so I thought. So I then put everything away and flushed the commode. I thought it would all go down, and it would be OK, but it didn't go down. It formed a huge wet cloud and came up all over the bathroom and me. I tried to wipe it up, but it wouldn't stop coming out of the commode. I knew I was in so much trouble. Right after that, I heard Momma coming down the hall. It was fun, but now it was over. "Chris, when I find you in these suds, I'm going to whoop your little ass."

I don't want to talk about that spanking anymore. Moving on, I love the music! Babyface is at his best. Motown is putting the radio on fire with Anita Baker, Freddie Jackson, Aretha Franklin, Gerald Levert, and Patti Labelle. Yes, I know something about Marvin Gaye, Miki Howard, Maze, Teena Marie, and Rick James. Betty Wright has come out with my favorite song, "No Pain, No Gain." You don't want me to get started on the gospel music Momma is playing when she is cooking in the kitchen!

Christina and I both love music. Even though I cannot say the words of a song, she knows that I am enjoying the music with her. She pulls me up to the mirror so we can watch ourselves sing. Christina is holding the end of her hairbrush up to my mouth while the boy part is playing. Then she switches it back to her mouth for the girl part. This goes on for hours at a time. Because Christina is singing with me, it makes me think that maybe some of my words are coming out right, even though my ears are only hearing grunts and moans. Maybe Christina knows that I am alive inside this body I feel locked into. As I try hard to say every word, I can feel my legs and arms flying everywhere, but I cannot stop them. As I try to say these words and keep up with the song, my stroller rocks back and forth. Christina seems to enjoy how excited I'm getting. She doesn't know that I am also laughing inside at how many times the barrette on the end of her plaits slaps her on the face while she's singing and shaking her head back and forth.

No one knows it, but I am paying attention to everything. I am aware of what is going on around me, and I hear what is said even though those who are talking don't think I "get it" (and would probably never say some of the things they say if they knew that I could understand it all). I don't think any of my brothers or sisters are hearing and seeing what I am getting from the adults around me. Of course, they wouldn't. They are normal. They are not broken like I am. All of this must be OK for someone like me.

There are so many things I do not like about the cold, hard, metal-and-leather that aligns my body from my hips all the way down to my heels, called braces. They always pinch me. I have bruises and scratches all over. They are stopping me from bending or turning. I feel like a robot. My legs and back are always rubbing against the metal. That is why I have sores and bumps all over me. They are stopping me from getting around. It is already hard for me to crawl around, but now I have these braces holding me down.

What bothers me most about the braces is that they make me stand out even more than I already do. I am trying to fit in and look as normal as possible. Braces make this hard. I went to the mall with Momma and Paul to buy me some new shoes, Reeboks. While we were trying on shoes, another kid was looking at me. I mean he looked at me for a long, long time. I'm sure he was trying to figure out why I was in a stroller and not walking around like he was. Then all of a sudden, his mom grabbed him by the arm and jerked him as she said, "Stop looking at him!" "What's wrong with looking at me? He just wanted to know why I was in the stroller, right? Or is it because I am some kind of freak or alien like I see on TV sometimes? Things like this make me hate being in public. I wonder if my brothers and sisters are ashamed of me.

I am back at school again. Being here feels different than it ever felt before. All of the pictures and ABCs are removed from the wall. I can smell used diapers, smoke, and coffee. I never really wanted to come here in the first place, but now I hate this place. I want to go home and never come back.

I have a new teacher, Mrs. Smith. She doesn't care about any of us. Mrs. Smith pays the others and me no attention. Sometimes she does not give us anything to eat during the day or change our pants. My mom and brothers think I dirtied my pants during my ride home from school. That is just not the truth. The teacher did not take the time to put me in a clean set of clothes. It seems like Mrs. Smith is tired and mad, so she is taking it out on us.

Mrs. Smith makes me a part of her smoking breaks. Every day, we go into the bathroom that is attached to the classroom. With the flick of the light switch, the light comes on and I hear the sound of a running fan over my head. This place is nothing like my home. It is always dirty and smelly. I see the garbage can in the corner overflowing with trash. This would never be the case in my home. As she rolls me up to the sink, she fills it up with water while jumping up on the counter, facing me and allowing her feet to hang off the floor. She starts taking puffs of her cigarette and then pushes my head under the water. I can feel the water run down my neck and into my shirt. Every time she lets me up, I look up at Mrs. Smith as she stares at the ceiling and blows her smoke into the air. Why is she doing this? Is this what happens when you are the way I am? Is it OK for her to do this because of what I am?

When I am not with my teacher during her smoking breaks or in therapy, I spend several hours of my day sitting in the corner, staring at white walls. While looking at the walls, I wonder what my life will be like. What is going to happen to me? What if my momma dies? Could my brothers take care of me? I just want to get out of these braces and this stroller. I want to crawl around and be free for once.

When I'm not in school, I spend a lot of time with my older cousin, James. He takes me places and does a lot of things with me. While we are together, James rolls up grass in white paper and smokes it. I've also seen him do the same thing with a pipe. I have watched him create what he calls "mushroom tea." I know this is not good because I hear Mom warning my brothers of this drink all the time. After making the tea, we go into the living room. He parks my stroller right beside the couch where he is sitting and starts to watch a movie. The only time I see a movie like this is when I am with James. The men and women aren't wearing clothes and are very close to one another.

I do not like my mom's new boyfriend, Lee. Momma does not drink or smoke, but she is in love with Lee, who does these things all the time. I hate the way he treats her. I feel like she thinks he is going to change his ways. I can tell by the looks on their faces that my brothers and sisters have a problem with him as well. All of us want her to be happy. With every tear that rolls down Momma's face because of his mistreatment, I can feel my heart getting tighter and tighter toward him. Lee makes it hard for me to be trapped in this body. Now that the argument is over, I can literally feel the emotional attempts from everyone to get our environment back to some type of normalcy.

My momma asks her sisters to babysit me sometimes while she goes to work. By the way they call my name and smile at me, it seems they are excited to watch me and help out. But as soon as Momma gets into the car and out of the driveway, they start to bad-mouth her to me, calling her all kinds of names and saying things like, "If she didn't want kids, she should have never had y'all." They get mad when I use the bathroom on myself or when I slobber on their couch. When these things happen, they make me sit outside until they are ready to change me or just spank me for slobbering on their couch. They really hate feeding me at lunchtime. They say all the time; "Your mother is going to pay me back for this damn apple I'm giving you."

Something happened today that I will never understand. Another person thought it was OK to hurt me. As Roy comes closer to me, I can smell the same stuff on his breath, as Lee. He makes me very sick just by being in the room. There is something evil about the way he rubs my arms and his eyes go over my body. His heart seemed to beat faster and faster with happiness as mine beat faster and faster with fear and sadness. He left the room happy, but I lay here with the feeling of shame. I can't wait for my mom to come and get me away from him. I thought my life was hell before, but I was wrong. This—what is going on now—is hell.

I know what's going on, but I don't understand why it is happening. I am always thinking about everything that is going on around me. I do not want to continue to live my life like this. This is why I love music so much. The singers are singing about pain, love, and confusion. They are putting into words what I am feeling. This is amazing to me. How can someone that knows nothing about me sing about my feelings so well? Mahalia Jackson really knows my heart right now. She is singing a song that admits to her desire to be with the Lord and away from the heartaches, pain, and disappointments of this world. Inside, I am crying with Mahalia for the Lord to lead me home. I am tired of living in this fleshly cage they call body. I don't want to die. I just want to be free, however that may come to be.

Your Moment with America's Unconfined Life Coach, Motivational Speaker, Author, and Confidence Builder:

Wanting to escape does not make a person suicidal. It may mean that person is aware that they are not totally free. They know something or someone is holding them captive.

What is it you want to escape from?
Do you want to escape in order to give up on life or be released to live your life?
What would you do if you were free?

CHAPTER 4

Especially the Disabled

The Voice of Understanding: Christopher

No doubt about it Chris was going through a lot. It's hard to look back and see what he had to go through in order to become Christopher, the man who is writing this book today. I, Christopher, know now that God never creates anything He doesn't plan on using. Chris only saw the circumstances that he was in. Where I, Christopher, now see how God used those circumstances to do something magnificent in my life and the lives of those around me. So as you continue to read through the trails and tribulations Chris had to face don't get discouraged. You must remember that Christopher is here too. That means Chris has survived. Chris's longing for freedom is not a desire to die; it is a hunger to live. The desire to escape comes out of his fear of remaining confined. Chris was living in captivity, removed from society. He did not want to continue to live like that. Hanging in between the two was torture. He committed no crime to justify a life of torture.

The outside world didn't understand my language at that time. They just chalked up the noise I was making as a reaction because of my disability. I believe they thought to themselves, *Surely someone that had cerebral palsy and is classified as mentally disabled cannot be trying to communicate to us.* Now is a good time to address one important issue. I know there are people today wondering how much I really do remember. Let me answer that. I remember all of it—teachers, friends of the family, aunts, uncles, and older cousins. Chris heard and saw *everything* that was done and said in his presence. Just to be clear, what Chris, the boy, didn't understand then, Christopher, the man, understands now. Many people played a significant role in turning the body Chris was confined to into a cage he was locked and tortured in. I cannot live my life in denial of what happened.

However, Chris and I successfully kept all of this from my family for years. Why? I grew up in an era where you just don't talk about things like this. People of that time just swept it under the rug. They hid it in the corner. You get over it. You deny that it ever happened. You definitely don't talk about it. You just move on with your life. If you don't deny it, then everyone else around you will deny it. They will say, "You are making it up," rather than deal with the fact that something happened, inappropriately, on their watch.

In other words, thanks to the influence of a dysfunctional society, it is more important to appear to be normal than it is to take the steps to become normal. In order to become normal, people have to admit that something went wrong somewhere along the way. Back then, the saying was, "What goes on in this house stays in this house." That saying traps people from receiving the healing they need to move forward in life. Many parents wonder why their kids grow up and live a life contrary to the way they think they raised them. Unfortunately, I know from experience that the saying "What goes on in this house stays in this house," forces young adults to find a way to cope with their pain rather than dealing with it. Many times they run to drugs, alcohol, and sex as a way of escaping from the issues. The commandment of keeping it quiet has given Satan free reign to have a foothold on that person's life from that day forward.

With this in mind, I must tell you, as my story unfolds, you will gain knowledge of things I've done right and of things I have done wrong. Many people who knew me before may say to themselves, "He is not who I thought he was." They would be correct, but I am who I portray myself to be. I never said I was a sinless man. And most of all, I am not excusing myself from the penalty of my mistakes. But I honestly think life would have been quite different and easier if society had not related to me according to the disabled boy I was and instead treated me like the man I, just like any other boy, could become.

No doubt about it, my mom is not going to react well to what I am sharing in this book. One of her biggest concerns would be how what I'm writing will affect the lives of the people who did not treat Chris like they should have. Even though I did not mention actual names of these individuals and tried hard to protect those closest to me, she is going to say, "Don't you think people can figure that bleep out? Did you consider that?" And my answer is, "I have considered these individuals way more than they have ever considered Chris." With that in mind, I don't feel bad. They decided to take a risk. They did things to him and around him, betting that I would never be able to communicate what Chris was experiencing. They lost, just like 90 percent of the people who betted against me at that time of my life. I claim no responsibility for another man's gambling habits.

So no, I am not holding back in sharing my story. I will put everything on the table. Everyone that has something to hide ends up living in the same closet that his skeletons live in. Writing this book is not a claim of freedom. It is a declaration of freedom. I am going to live with an unconfined heart, soul, and mind. I will no longer hide what I think, ignore what I feel, and subdue my beliefs. My story is raw and straightforward because life has rubbed directly up against me, causing me to develop some sores that I cannot hide.

I often wonder what people were thinking back then. Did they not understand as a boy I already had to deal with the insecurities of a disability and coming to terms with it? Why did they do and say things that made me feel even worse about who I was? Did they know how much their actions would delay and confuse my pursuit for a life of freedom? It seemed like everyone outside of my home hated me. The sad part is over time that little boy in me, Chris, would adopt their feelings. His environment and society labeled him as retarded and made him feel worthless. I know that "retarded" is not the correct terminology for people who actually just have a mental disability, but I want you to be aware of the label Chris had to overcome.

I got so tired of the violence in my home. When Lee was drunk, it became a total nightmare. The doors slamming, glass breaking, people yelling, and the profanity that expresses nothing but hate made me so nervous. When I hear those noises, I am reminded of violence. Even today, I find myself jumping and cringing inside when I hear a loud noise on TV on a normal and calm day. The ruckus I was tired of was not only at home. I got tired of seeing my older brothers, Paul and Lamont, constantly fighting with other boys in the neighborhood. I wish I didn't have to experience so much hostility. It seems like this was a part of life in that community. People were so angry with other people as well as themselves that they could only express it through angry emotions.

Chris wondered for a long time if mom would come back from her dates with her boyfriend happy in a good mood. He knew if her boyfriend had too much to drink his Mom wouldn't happy with him. My mom's relationship with this man still affects my life today. I can't believe that love can be this powerful, but I can't blame her. I have no idea what she needed in order to get through raising seven kids on her own.

Also, I know times were hard back in those days, but no one in my family was so poor that they could not afford to feed a child every now and then. Knowing my mom, she probably tried to pay her sisters for babysitting me, but they would not take it, even though they felt like she owed them.

When I think about the environment my cousin put Chris in, it baffles me. Even if he knew, beyond a shadow of a doubt, that Chris did not comprehend the things he was doing, any moron should know better than to expose a boy that age to those things. Now I know the meaning of the saying "A mind is a terrible thing to waste." Chris's mind in his motionless body was more productive than his cousin's mind in a fully able body.

Chris's teacher at that time was just crazy. There is no other way I can explain it or come to terms with the things she was doing. All I can think is that she found it entertaining to be cruel to Chris because she knew he could not speak out.

It's still hard today to think about Roy, whose actual name will forever remain anonymous. Mentally, Chris rejected what he was going through, but physically, Roy had absolute freedom to do whatever he wanted. Unfortunately, this abuse went on for many years. He successfully planted fear of what might happen if Chris ever spoke up. In 2011, the U.S. Department of Justice reported that a crime among people with disabilities is likely to go unreported for many reasons such as mobility and communication barriers, social or physical isolation of the victim, a victim's normal feeling of shame or self-blame, ignorance of the justice system, or the predator is a family member or primary caregiver.

I knew I was getting better. I have been able to move around on my knees from room to room for a while now. My family even understands some of my attempts to verbalize. Nevertheless, society treats the disadvantaged as if they are used, recycled, or useless. Chris felt like he was worthless. Everything he did was out of that worthless feeling. Chris spent years of his life trying to prove these feelings, while I, Christopher, spent years of my life trying to disprove these feelings. The things I have shared and will continue to share will forever affect my life.

I was becoming mentally and emotionally neuropathic. This happens when an individual becomes numb to what they are feeling inside. For a long time, the boy in me, Chris, denied the hurt others have done to us. Our wounds became infected by our refusal to pay attention to the pain. I have learned that it's more damaging to be numb to the pain than it is to feel the pain. Chris and I refuse to acknowledge what has happened to us all those years. And from that point way up until my adulthood, everything was the outcome of the internal pain we never dealt with. We thought our actions were a Band-Aid over the wound, but in reality, we were constantly picking on a sore spot, making it worse than it was before. The pain that we were ignoring was causing Chris to become bitter, mean, and draw deeper into the corner of our cage.

Your Moment with America's Unconfined Life Coach, Motivational Speaker, Author, and Confidence Builder:

It is so easy to become mentally and emotionally neuropathic. Pain is a hard thing to deal with when it is deep within. When people try to hold their feelings inside, that pain has more control over them than they have over the pain.

Have you been hurt by a person, thing, or event?
Has your life of freedom been delayed and confused by a person, thing, or event?
Has your past paralyzed you?

CHAPTER 5

Why, What, Where, Will?

The Voice of Understanding: Christopher

My aunts and others are so lucky I couldn't tell Mom of the things they were doing to me. It would have been hell for everyone. Everybody is always saying that Momma is so sweet, and they can't wait to meet her. She sounds like a wonderful lady and mother. And I tried to give them an accurate picture of her. I just don't know if they believe me or not. They still insist that they can't wait to meet her. When they make this request, I am thinking in my head, *She will like you as long as you do, say, and act the way she expects you to. You fall off the script, and your ass is grass. She is the lawnmower.*

The Voice of Experience: Chris

"Christopher, where are you? We have to go *now!*" I hear Momma calling as she grabs her keys and mumbles a couple of cusswords under her breath. "When I get down to that school, I'm going to kick some ass." Oh no, I know what that means. Paul or Lamont did something that they shouldn't have done and the teacher called. Momma doesn't put up with stuff like this. She always says that she doesn't have time to take off work to follow up on "shit like this." Lamont or Paul is going to really get a beating from Momma. The more I think about it; I hope it is them that she is all riled up about. She has some love for her kids, but if she finds out that it is something one of the teachers did, she is going to tear that school apart. I know because I have seen her do it several times, especially at my sister's school.

The other day, I got into trouble. I didn't mean to. I thought I was doing the right thing. Momma loaded me up in the car and hit the pedal with her foot to make the car warm up. Then she went back around my grandmother's house to our trailer. I thought it would be a good idea if I kept it warmed up for her. So I lifted my left leg and braces over the hump of the car and pressed on the pedal. As I gently pressed the pedal, the car made a loud growling noise. That was so cool. I decided to do it again, and again, and again. I did not know that smoke was coming up around the car. I was totally focused on what I was doing. Then suddenly my mom opened the car door and slapped my knee really hard. I pulled it back as quickly as I could. She yelled at me with a cussword. It made me very mad when she slapped my knee. I wasn't trying to be bad. I just thought this was fun. It was also something that needed to be done, and I could do it.

What is going on? Whoa! I feel like I am going to throw up. These men are quickly moving me from my bed to a bed-on-wheels. Why are they running with me through the house? My momma doesn't allow people to run in the house! Why are they doing this?

Wait. They are taking me away. I hear the sound of the wheels from the bed going over the cracks in the sidewalk as we run from the front door of my home, around the side of my grandmother's house and to the driveway where a big loud van is waiting for me. They are quickly opening the door and sliding me into the back of the van.

"Where is Momma? Are they taking me away? Where is Momma?" I thought. I always knew this would happen. I always felt like my momma would be so much better off if she did not have to take care of me. I knew it was hard for her. I have been waiting for the day

that she would drop me off somewhere and leave. Every morning when I got on the bus, I daydreamed as I watched the lift fold and the doors shut. I would dream that the bus came to take me away from my home. I can hear myself crying to Momma and begging to the driver not to take me away. I imagine her looking down at the ground as tears went down her face. Is this finally going to happen?

There she is. She is getting into the van with me, but she seems just as worried and confused as I am. What's going on? I wish I could tell them to stop and leave me alone, but I can't. With a jerk, I feel the van move and hear the loud engine accelerate. They are quickly taking me from my home to the emergency room.

Now that we are here, they are quickly moving me from the bed-on-wheels to another bed. There is too much is going on around me. People are poking and pulling on me. Why are all these wires and tubes all over me now? I can hear my momma crying in the back of the room. She says, "Oh, my baby!" I know she is talking about me. Lights out. Things go dark in my world. Four days later, I am back. I have had seizures before, but none like this. I am so tired and weak. Why do these things always happen to me? Why me?

I'm back home now. Lee, my mom's boyfriend, continues his behavior. It cuts my chest like a knife. Will she ever get tired of him? She tries to constantly make everything just right for him. But no matter how perfect it is, within a few drinks, he starts to cuss and fuss; and it all goes downhill from there. How can such a strong woman be so weak?

Lee comes into my room to tell me that I am the reason he is so angry today. I'm not surprised. I believe my family would be a whole lot better off if I had not been born. The fact that I always need them is getting to be too much. I know Paul and Lamont want to go outside and play football and hang out with the rest of the kids, but they can't, because of me. My sisters are aggravated, because every time I need something to eat or drink, they have to stop whatever they are doing and give it to me. My momma has to spend so much time driving me to doctor's appointments, therapy appointments, speech appointments, and so on. We spend one day in the emergency room and the next day out. We will go back again. So what Lee says only proves what I already believe. It is my fault. But why does it hurt so badly? It is almost as if I'm hoping it's not true, even though I can understand why and believe it is the truth. **Why is it easier for me to believe the worst about myself, even though that belief is not what I feel in my heart?**

I know that my momma's sisters do not like babysitting me. The way they continue to treat me and talk about her makes it so obvious. I can't understand why they are agreeing to watch me if they have so much hatred toward her. Also, I wonder why this one aunt threatens, "to beat my ass" if I ever tell my momma what she is doing and saying around me. I can't talk that well anyway, so why is she telling *me* this?

My sisters still don't understand my disability. Neither do I. But they are so cruel to me at times. Angela gets mad at me because Paul made her stop what she was doing and fix me lunch. I eat and drink a lot. I don't know why, but I do. So Angela, out of her anger, called me a dog that crawls around on all fours. I just so happened to be sitting next to a box of canned dog food that belongs to Tiger. I didn't think about it. I just grabbed a can and threw it at her as she turned and walked away. It was a good throw, if I must say so myself. I bet she'll think twice before she says that to me again. When they say these things, it really hurts my feelings. I don't know how else to respond because I know it's true. I really want to be normal like them. **"Where do I go from here?"**

I am still hanging around my cousin, and I actually like him. He is someone outside my immediate family that wants to spend time with me. I don't quite understand why he is allowing me to see some of the things that I am seeing. The movies he is playing on TV makes me, feel in my heart, that what Roy is doing to me is not right. I feel that stuff like this is only for a boy and a girl. All I can do now is cry when I think of it. Everyone in the house doesn't understand why I am crying so much, but I just do not like being around Roy. I am starting to feel for the first time the effects of hatred in the heart. **Will things ever change?**

The Voice of Understanding: Christopher

Back to the questions, "Why me? What now? Where do I go from here? Will things ever change? Why is it easier for me to believe the worst about myself even though that belief is contrary to what I feel in my heart and soul?" In order for me to find my answers, I had to face society head on. It's a fact: I was born into a society that accepts and rejects new members based on their label—white, black, able, disabled, rich, poor. Whatever label they decide is best for me is the one that I will live with for the rest of my life.

I know it was important for me to understand my disability and the significant role it would play in my life. It was equally important for me to understand society and the significant role they too would play in my life. I knew whether I liked it or not, they were going to point out my weaknesses and decide how much value I was going to bring to their table. Therefore, I had to be aware of their weaknesses and decide how much value they would bring to the table in my life, as well. If society was going to point out things that give them justification in labeling me "disabled," then I had to be aware of their shortcomings and be able to see how dysfunctional they are. Anyone that is allowing another person to speak into their lives has to be aware and take account of that person's weaknesses.

So with that in mind, anyone who labels a person's weakness, illness, or uniqueness and uses it as an excuse to devalue that person takes away his or her rights to pursue a full life. Furthermore, anyone who shuns them into the corner of life is dysfunctional. We have to look at the reality of this situation. I personally believe there is something wrong with society, when their inability to support and adjust to the uniqueness of a person becomes justification for casting people with disabilities aside. They are operating out of an abnormal mind-set. One would think society should be a group of individuals who are able to function in a diverse environment. A fully functional society is able to use the unique gifts and talents of any member of their society.

To go back and find me worthy now, society has to reevaluate the boundaries that they set for me. This requires an admission that the value they initially place on my life is not actually accurate. Rather than admitting they are wrong, I feel like they continue to define me and confine me based on things they can't understand. Even though society communicated to me that I had no premise to believe that I would be anything more than a person trapped inside my own body, I pursued my dream of a normal life. I knew that freedom would never come without a change. Somehow I had to pull something positive out of my negative situation.

> *"It was the best of times it was the worst of times"*
> (Charles Dickens).

What does this really mean? How can someone look at the worst point of their life and come out with the impression that it was also the best time of their life? There was obviously a change in the middle of the storm that the writer was elaborating on. Something happened that has caused his view on that situation to change. If the worst times of a person's life bring about change, and that change brings forth growth and they are able to identify, recognize, and utilize that growth, then couldn't that be considered the best times of their life? While waiting for the change, if we fail to grow, then the change becomes obsolete. It is the growth that happens in the midst of a change that helps our lives to move forward. A change with the same mind-set and the same ideas about life will eventually get that person right back where they started. When we are able to grow and learn through that transformation, the change is beneficial.

"Why me? What now? Where do I go from here? Will things ever change?" These are not just questions of vulnerability; these are questions of identity. Who you are called to be is revealed through your weaknesses. Why, because no one goes to God questioning what they perceive to be as strength. No one asks God, "Why am I so rich? Why am I so intelligent? Why am I blessed so much in my life?" Though God has a purpose behind even the blessings, we do not question it. We question and complain about only what we perceive as weakness. These questions call us to constantly get in the ring and wrestle with God. I believe this is one of the many ways His purpose for our life is revealed.

Your Moment with America's Unconfined Life Coach, Motivational Speaker, Author, and Confidence Builder:

In order to begin breaking away from the thing that keeps you trapped, you must begin to investigate your life. The knowledge of knowing how you got there will be instrumental in breaking free from it.

Do you naturally believe the worst about yourself?
Take a selfish moment, look at the things that you wish you could change in your life, and ask yourself, "Why?"
What would it take to change the "why me?" answers to information that empowers you to move forward?
Where do you go from here?

CHAPTER 6

Prepare for a Change

The Voice of Experience: Chris

Right now, I love the song "A Change Is Gonna Come" by Sam Cooke. I'm not the only one that is fighting for a change. Now I have people in my life that want to see me get better. At least three times a week, I have three ladies coming in my classroom to work with only me. The first one tells me it's time for physical therapy. She constantly stretches and pulls every part of my body, over and over again. After that, she is trying to get me to crawl from one side of the room to the other. Sometimes I just don't feel like it, but I do it anyway because I know this is helping me to achieve my goals. For me, it is the beginning of getting out of this body I am trapped in, and I am willing to work for it.

The other lady wants me to move blocks around and reach out for things she puts in front of me. I think the name of this is occupational therapy. At least that's what I heard my teacher call it. She aggravates me the most because I just can't do the things she is asking me to do. It makes me feel like what I am doing is not good enough, but I am going to try it anyway.

And, finally, I have speech therapy. It seems like this takes hours of my day. The therapist is asking me to make the same sounds that she is making. I have a hard time when she asks me to say sounds like st, sk, sc, sm, and sl. For some reason, I just can't get these sounds out of my mouth. I am watching her lips, and I am doing my best to make my mouth move the same way, but I just can't do it. I hear my therapists tell my mom all the time that I am one of the most determined kids they have ever worked with. I am not sure what that means, but I will not stop trying to do my best.

Now that I am home, it seems like therapy starts back up again. Mom is now constantly correcting me. "Chris, sit up," she says as she pushes my body to the left. "Chris, hold your head up. Chris, pull your feet back." Doesn't she understand that I am just tired and worn out from the day? A part of me wants to stop and not even try anymore, but I know that this is helping me. If I want to be able to play with my brothers and sisters, I have to learn how to do these things. I really want to be able to move around like they can. So no matter how hard Mom pushes me, I will always do my best to do what she asks. The good part about my hard work is Mom treats me to McDonalds as often as she can. She tells me not to tell my brothers and sisters. I don't know why she says that because all I can do for now is make sounds. I am not able to speak out loud yet, but everyone talks to me as if I can talk back to them. I like this. It makes me feel as if I am part of their world.

I have my first manual wheelchair, and I really enjoy going fast. Paul and I go out for a run all the time. It is such an exciting feeling. Paul lifts my front wheels off the ground, tipping me back just far enough to see his face as he runs. The combination of having the wind blowing in my face, hearing Paul's feet pounding the pavement, his heavy breathing, and the wheels of my wheelchair grinding into the ground at rapid speed relaxes me so much that I almost fall asleep. I love it when Paul looks down at me while he is running. I hope he can tell by my smile that I love every minute of it. He must know that because he smiles back every time. It feels like we ran forever, but I can't wait to do it again.

Today I am having so much fun! A friend of my brother and sister is pushing me full speed from the park back to the house. The other kids are way behind us, and we are going to beat them to the driveway for sure. But this feels a little bit different from when Paul is running with me. He always has my front wheels off the ground. My front wheels are on the ground now, so it's a little bit shakier as we are running. I just felt a bump. I don't think he has control of my chair anymore. We are so close to the finish line, but my left wheel is off the ground. Oh no, I'm going to fall right into this ditch! Now I know why Paul keeps my front wheels up in the air. And so here I am, headfirst in a ditch. I can smell the cold, wet gunk that is all over me. They finally got me out, and I'm covered in mud from my head to my toes. My wheelchair is just as muddy as I am, and Russell is freaking out. I wonder if he knows that I am enjoying every bit of this. I think he's worried that I am hurt, but I'm not! I can't stop smiling.

After getting me up and back into my chair, Russell knows, just like I know, that I cannot go into my mom's house like this. She would kill us if she knew they were running in the streets with me. But even more importantly, we cannot take the risk of getting mud all over the house! Russell has to do something to save everyone's butt. So he takes me behind my grandmother's house. After getting there, he sprays me off with a hose. I am freezing! But this is so much fun! I actually got to hang out with my brothers, sisters, and their friends. I can't remember a time that I felt like I was truly part of the gang.

I have a new teacher now, and this guy loves his job. He enjoys being around his students. I can tell he knows that there is life inside of this body. He is spending so much time with my best friend and me. My best friend is different too. Whatever his problem is, he's able to do more than I can. Our teacher is so cool. He spends lots of hours of the day reading stories, going outside for recess, and just talking to us like we're normal people. The other day, he got in trouble by the principal. The teacher and his aide were taking us for a walk down the sidewalk in front of the school. I don't think he had permission from her to do that, so she chewed him out right there. But I get the sense he will do it all again when the time is right.

It seems like everything is going good in spite of the bad stuff. I'm OK with the level of activity I'm having with the outside world. My teacher, my physical therapist, my brothers, sisters, and their friends are all very friendly and are allowing me to be a part of their world. I'm just not happy with one thing. There's still something that is not right. After school each day, my brothers and sisters are spending hours with their books. Paul and Lamont seem to be in a hurry to finish whatever they are doing so they can go outside and play. Dewayne and Russell seem to be OK with taking their time. For Angela and Christina, it looks like just a fun game that they are playing. Whatever it is, I want to figure out what they are doing with these books.

I know what I'm going to do. When everyone goes to sleep, I'm going to look in Christina's book sack. After dragging her book sack into the bathroom and locking the door, I pull out this colorful book and open it. I have no idea what it says, but I recognize the pictures. I know what a cat is and what a dog is. And the letters and shapes are just like the letters and shapes I see on TV. So this C stands for cat, and this B stands for ball. And if it's not right, who cares? It seems fun to me. I'm just going to pretend I know what I am looking at.

Every night in this bathroom, I am able to make up a world of my own. The more books I find, the more new characters, places, and things are a part of my world. But I want more stuff to bring into my imaginary world. So I'm going to start collecting the papers that Mom puts in the garbage after she opens the mail. A lot of the numbers and words fit into this world. I love watching *Sesame Street* too. They also have letters and numbers every day that sound just like the words I am using in my made-up world. And my teacher is reading books a lot like the ones I take out of my sister's book bag at night. It seems right to me, but I will never tell anyone because I know I am making it all up. The best part about this made-up world of mine is that I am OK in it. No one makes me feel as if I don't belong here.

The Voice of Understanding: Christopher

I've developed a deep passion to be in an environment where I am fully accepted. That was the passion that I was hanging on to. However, I didn't know there were three different guards holding me captive: my label, the society I lived in, and the church. I just knew something had to change. I was fighting for that change. When someone is pursuing the possibility of a change, they also free themselves up to dream. They know that a change can bring on new possibilities for their life. Maybe Chris's made-up world was actually my dream.

The disabled label severely damaged my self-esteem. I grew up thinking that my disability made me less than the next person. I now realize that the mind can be our worst enemy. It took me years to rise above the suppression of the label. I found no comfort in being who I was. An internal ego conflict started inside of me. This is when the mind, heart, or soul becomes defensive because it feels like it has been attacked by society. Society told Chris one thing; but I, Christopher, believed another. I saw some light, some signs of hope in the progress I was making. At least that's what I told myself.

I have learned that a person who cannot see the light at the end of the tunnel is living a confined life. My life was so full of darkness that my ability to imagine light was the only way I knew I was still alive. I had to find something to hold on to. The little glimpses of light that I saw would not have lit up much for anyone else, but it brought me enough hope to light up my whole world. I took any positive thing or good vibes as vital signs that indicated that I still had life in me.

Unfortunately, my family and close circle of friends were the only ones that saw the vital signs as signs of life. Everybody else saw me as brain dead, therefore useless. Chris felt like the person he could become and the things he could achieve were irrelevant if society did not agree with it. It seemed like no matter what he did to demonstrate that there was more to him, society would continue to treat him as if he was indeed worthless. Chris and I had to learn that people categorize and label other people based on what they do not understand rather than acknowledging their ignorance.

Someone once said that you would notice a change in yourself long before the people around you notice the change. It seemed like society made up their minds that I was an invalid. "You should not be here. They will not understand you. You are disabled and not as important as the next person. No one really loves you. They just tolerate you. You will never be good enough." These are thoughts I struggle with every day of my life. Where does a low self-esteem come from? No one is born with a low self-esteem. It comes from rejection.

The signs of freedom were either ignored or covered up by the actions of the people around me.

Chris allowed society's views of a person with a disability to convince him that we would never be sufficient. Society was an infectious disease that further weakened our condition. The low self-esteem that I, Christopher, deal with today was inherited from Chris and was forced on him by society. Society has become my wheelchair. Their actions forced Chris to live in his made-up world, especially when things got hard. There were times it did not matter what his abuser was doing to him, what his mom's boyfriend was up to, or how kids made him feel on the playground; he would just stay in his little world. In this world, Chris felt normal and accepted.

I cannot deny that my childhood will continue to play a significant role in my life. There is nothing more damaging to the soul than bottled-up hatred and hurt. You will find that this is the root of bitterness, insecurities, and unjustified anger. When a person puts on a mask, he often gets into the character of that mask. He begins to act like the person that the mask says he is. If you were to wear that mask long enough, sooner or later, you will run out of lines. At that point, what is beneath that surface, up underneath the mask, will come to light. So I put on the mask and I did my best to know my lines. I put on Chris's face and tried to be happy in this mask. I was just a boy who found a way to escape from his circumstances.

The made-up world that Chris and I lived in for so long was a place of escape for Chris, but it was an incubator for me. It protected me from my environment long enough to heal and become the man who is writing these words today.

Your Moment with America's Unconfined Life Coach, Motivational Speaker, Author, and Confidence Builder:

Everyone will face rejection in life. Sometimes that rejection will make us put on a mask and hide. However, in these moments, we have to check our own vital signs and find glimpses of light in darkness.

Are you prepared for the change you are waiting for?
Do you have the freedom to dream?
Are you keeping your dreams protected?

CHAPTER 7

The Imaginary World

The Voice of Experience: Chris

It's Saturday morning, and I know Mom is at work; but in the air, I can smell boiled wieners, chili mixed with ketchup and mustard, and toast. This tells me two things: one, we are out of hot dog buns, and two, Lamont is in the kitchen. He is pretty good at looking around and making a meal out of whatever we have around the house. Paul and Lamont have taken on the responsibility of not being the man in the house but being assistant parents to my mom. I can tell that they feel a sense of responsibility in making sure that my sisters, other brothers, and myself are well taken care of. When it comes to my mom, my two youngest brothers, and my two sisters, Paul and Lamont are very concerned and have a lot of compassion. Paul and Lamont quickly step in when Mom or one of us is sick. Momma recently had surgery and could not get herself in or out of the chair. Paul literally had to bathe her and dress her every day for a week and a half. He seemed to do it without even blinking an eye. And I can tell by how gentle he is toward her than he truly loves her. I have felt both Paul's and Lamont's love as well through the way they have taken care of me.

I am kind of hungry, so I am going to make my way out of the bed, down the hall, and to the living room. As I slide out of my bed onto the cold brown linoleum, I can hear the subfloor cracking because of the added weight of my small body. If I sit here long enough, I can feel a slight draft coming through the corners of the floor. As I move from room to room, I count the number of holes and tears in the linoleum. Every day it seems like I discover one more hole or tear. In every room, the patterning and coloring change, however, the stability and temperature of the floors remain the same.

Before I can get there, Paul scoops me up really quick, throws me on the couch, and begins tickling me. He does it so much. I can't stand it. I want him to stop. But at the same time, I love it and I don't want him to stop. But I know how I can get him to stop. I can always say, "Pee." He knows that I have a difficult time holding it, so that works. When I don't start crawling toward the restroom, he starts all over again.

When Momma got home, I got in trouble, but it really wasn't my fault. They asked for it. I was sitting there under the carport at my grandmother's house, and the kids from next-door came over. They started hitting me behind my head and making the same noise that I make as I am trying to talk. They really made me mad, and I felt like I had to somehow let them know how I felt about this. So I tried hard to hold up my right hand while folding back all of my fingers except for my middle finger. I wanted them to know what I felt about what they were doing to me. I wasn't sure I did it right until they went into the house and told my mom. She came outside and popped me on that same hand, so I guess they did know what I was trying to say. Oh well.

I would like to take you into my make-believe world, but I have to tell you something about it first. It is an "**if/then**" world. It all depends on where I am and what's going on around me. *If* I'm here and these things are happening, *then* I go into this type of world. And if I am there and those things are happening, then I go into this world. I never know when I wake up in the morning what world I'm going to play in that day.

One of my favorite scenes for my make-believe worlds is where Momma works. She cleans and irons for some very rich white people with huge houses. As soon as she goes upstairs, the downstairs is my playground. But my imaginary world starts when we first walk through the door. As soon as we get in the house, she sits me in front of the TV while she goes upstairs to make up beds and begin washing. As soon as I think she is completely upstairs, I begin to quickly take off my leg braces. They were just a cover-up to get me in. The moment I get out of these braces, I transform from a helpless, disabled boy to a private-eye detective. Now it's my job to go from room to room, finding information that is going to prove that the owner of this home is involved in a crime. As I crawl from room to room, I imagine myself walking into offices just like the cops on *Magnum PI* and *Hunter*. I pull out my imaginary gun, peep around the corner, then look around to make sure no one is in there before I crawl in. Once I am there, I open every drawer I can open. I look under every bed. I hear Momma calling me, but in my world, it is a warning sign that people are getting close and I have to get out. As soon as I get everything closed, Momma comes into the room and asks me, "What are you doing in here?" I just look up at her and try my best to say, "Nothing." At this point in my life, it seems like Momma, my brothers, and my sisters are beginning to pick up on one-word sentences I am trying to express. She gives me a "Yeah, right" suspicious look as she walks away. Thank God I have dodged that one. Let me keep investigating.

Soon Momma will be coming downstairs to iron. When that happens, I will gather up materials for my nighttime made-up world, just like I do when my aunts babysit me. Mom and her sisters love watching *Guiding Light*, *As the World Turns*, *Bold and the Beautiful*, and *The Young and the Restless*. There's something about *The Young and the Restless* I really like. Watching Jack and Victor battle over power and fame excites me. Every time I watch these shows, I use the characters as people in my imaginary world. The books that I am sneaking out of my sister's room at night are private documents and codes that I am pretending to figure out. They are top-secret information on Jack, Victor and their companies. Every time my mom puts junk mail in the garbage, I pretend that it's a secret document that someone has dropped off in the drop box for me to investigate. Nighttime for me was a world where I was a smart and ruthless businessman who was going to take over both Jack and Victor's companies.

In the evenings and on weekends, while my brothers, sisters, and cousins are playing in the front yard, I am on the porch with the older people. They have no idea that I'm hearing and understanding all that they are saying. I am literally a fly on the wall. They become a part of my imaginary world as well. Some of the things I hear and see them do are similar to the TV shows we are watching during the day. I know who is sleeping with who, who is stealing from who. And who is lying to who.

The days I go to the school, I imagine the bus as my limousine that picks me up to go to the office of the business that I own. The codes that I figured out the night before are now being used to expand my business and my goal to eventually take over the two companies. I now can connect my sister's books with the things that the teacher is reading to me as well as from speech class. When I go to physical and occupational therapy, I imagine myself doing something physically daring, like climbing out of a window or jumping from one car to the next.

To me, it is a lot easier to pretend that my life is full of fun and that I am actually able to move around than to feel what I am really feeling. In my make-believe world, no one dislikes me. I have absolute control of what is going on around me as well as my body. No one is forcing me to do, see, or hear things I don't want to do, see, or hear.

Every second that goes by, I feel like something is being taken away from me. Not only can I not stop him; I can't stop the feeling of my soul being sucked out of me. I hate this. I hate Roy. Does he know how sick he makes me when he does this? I hate the way he smells. I can't stand the sweat that is falling off his eyebrows. I am so tired of smelling his breath. And most of all, I am sick of the noise he makes. I wish he would just stop and leave me alone. I hate this. It makes me sick.

"If you ever tell a soul, I will kill you and your damn momma." Those words echoed inside of me for a long time. They were substitutes for the soul that was once in me. I've seen my mom hurt too much by Lee, to allow someone else to hurt her. I will never tell of these feelings and experiences. They will always be locked and buried within me.

"Many people with disabling conditions are especially vulnerable to victimization because of a real or perceived inability to fight back, notify others or testify about the victimization according to the U.S. Department of Justice" (the voice of understanding, Christopher).

My cousin, James, may be thinking that I am watching the trash that he is playing on TV, but I really have my own TV show playing in the back of my mind; and it's really much better than what he has on that screen. While all of the commotion is going on inside the house, I'm not sure what my mom, Lee, and the others think I am thinking. In my mind, I'm off in my imaginary world. I have decided not to take in the feelings from this fight. Most of the time, life is so much easier if I stay in this make-believe place.

I would rather be a part of their world than to have to make up my own, but I don't see how it is possible. I can't understand why I want to be a part of the real world. So here I am, stuck between the two worlds. I want to be a part of what I know is real; however. I am accepted into this other world and I don't have to deal with the pain that the real world makes me feel. Once again, I am feeling trapped, so I just want to get away from everyone for a little while.

I'm sitting here on the last step of my grandma's house, enjoying the smell of freshly cut grass and coming rain. I know I'm not supposed to be out here by myself. I'm pretty sure someone watched me crawl out. Because the grass was just cut, one of my cousins or uncles has to be behind the house washing off the lawnmower before putting it up. I'm sitting here thinking about tomorrow. It will be so much fun for everyone else. We will all go to church, come home, get out of our Sunday clothes, and eat a lot of food at my grandma's house, and then everybody will begin to look for Easter eggs, except for me. I will be sitting on the porch with the adults, either in my imaginary world, or watching my brothers, sisters, and cousins and wishing I could be a part of the real world.

I've been working so hard to get better. Why can't I talk like everyone else? Why am I so different from everybody else? What am I fighting for now? Tomorrow will just be another day where I sit and watch. I know my brothers and sisters will share what they found with me, but I won't have the fun of finding it myself. This makes me sad. Why am I trying so hard to get better?

I can't hold back the tears anymore. The thought of never being a part of the real world is really getting to me. I want so much just to be like everyone else. Why with every thought there are more tears coming down my face? I cannot stop crying. Oh no, Paul, my older brother, just turned the corner and sees me crying. "What's wrong, Buddy?" he says as he picks me up, while allowing my arms to wrap around his neck and my forehead to fall between his neck and shoulder.

As I cry even harder, I squeeze Paul with all my might, and in return, he squeezes me just as hard. For a moment, it feels like the door of my trap is open. My pain is trying to escape. At the same time, Paul's love for me is trying to come in. I'm trying to give Paul all the pain that I am feeling inside of me right now. And by the way he is hugging me back, I can tell he is trying to give me all the love that he has inside of him. Now I am not sure why I am crying. Is it because all of my thoughts and the way I feel about myself? Or is it just because I can't believe someone loves me this much in spite of who I am? My pain, Paul's love, the smell of freshly cut grass, and the incoming rain lets me know that this is the real world. This is really who I am. I cannot run away from this body that I feel trapped in. I just have to find a way to deal with it.

The Voice of Understanding: Christopher

I can't believe Chris shared the details of our make-believe world. I promised myself that I would never tell anyone. Yes, I am aware that most kids have an imaginary world. However, I think I was deeper and spent more time in this world than most kids. As Christopher, **I wonder if this imaginary world was just a fun activity or a method of coping with the knowledge of living in a real society that would not accept me as I am.** I wonder how many disabled or mentally ill people pretend to be a lot further gone than they really are? Why would they do this? Because they know they live in a society that will reject them because of their differences, no matter the degree of their disability or illness.

Now that Chris has let the cat out of the bag, let me give you some more details. First of all, in our imaginary world, Chris was always white. For some reason, he related success and a perfect life to a white culture. At that time, if you were watching TV, most of the actors were Caucasian. I went to work with my mom who cleaned these elaborate houses for wealthy white people. Then we would go back to the black community with small houses, raggedy cars, and a survival atmosphere. When you consider all that, you can begin to see how Chris' idea of success was colored white.

I never wanted to be on that front porch. I always wanted to be out there running around with the other kids. It is kind of weird going back home now and seeing some of those same people. I wonder if they realize how much I have retained from those moments on the front porch. They exposed me to some things that a ten-year-old boy should never be exposed to. The things I've overheard, seen, experienced, and have to continue to live with throughout the course of my life prove that we live in a messed-up world.

During the time of dealing with my disability and the reality of it, I went to church with some friends of my mom. Even then I felt they were taking time out with me because of a personal agenda rather than just wanting to spend time with our family. I believe this was more of an act of charity, if you will, on their part. In the middle of the service, they took me up to the altar. While standing there, in the husband's arms, and next to his wife, the pastor began to pray for us. He continued to pray as he laid hands on each of us. Then the wife fell to the floor like a board. When they brought me home that night, they told my mom I was walking. I knew that wasn't the truth. I was in his arms the whole time. However, when she said that, I responded in my mind and heart just like a normal ten-year-old boy would respond who had lived his whole life wanting to get up and walk.

At that point in my life, everything I was doing was for one reason and one reason only: I wanted to be normal. I wanted to be able to talk just as clearly as the next person. I wanted my body to move like everyone else's. I had a deep desire to do all of the things that my brothers and sisters were able to do. For me, it wasn't about trying to be accepted as I am. My mentality was, "I needed to become normal to be accepted." I didn't understand the reality of my situation.

I wanted to believe that God was communicating to me through her. From that night on, I held on even tighter to the idea of no longer being disabled one day. I don't know what that woman was drinking or smoking, but I did not take one step that night. I believe she was just doing what the church and her religion said were appropriate for my situation. The church teaches us that a boy with a disability needed to be able to walk, talk, and move like the rest of the congregation in order to be whole and approved by God. Now looking back, I realize that I wasn't the only one confining me to a fantasy world at that time.

A confined life is a life stuck between fantasy and reality. I believe it's OK to dream as long as the individual comes out of that dream with a desire to live. People should not live in a fantasy. A person that is living in a make-believe world is living a confined life. If people don't want to live in the midst of their reality, then they must find the courage to change that reality, but escaping into a fantasy is not the answer. Fantasies are sometimes used as the corner of life. People tend to mentally check out of the reality of their lives because they feel they have no purpose. This corner is the punishment for the lack of purpose they feel they have. Instead of trying to find their purpose, they act just like kids in time out. Then they choose to live the rest of their lives in a fantasy world until their time is up.

Your Moment with America's Unconfined Life Coach, Motivational Speaker, Author, and Confidence Builder:

A fulfilled life requires us to live in an if-then world. "'If" allows us to dream. "Then" forces us to a result. "If" you are not dreaming big, "then" you are not accomplishing much.

Are you living in the real world with no faith, a fantasy world with no truth, or are you on the fence?
What are you trying not to deal within your life?
Are you ignoring your wake-up calls in life?

CHAPTER 8

Refining Moments

The Voice of Experience: Chris

I can't believe I am about to say it. I should not say what I am about to say, but it is on the tip of my tongue, and I can't hold it back any more. "STOP!" Who said that? That wasn't me, was it? I guess it was. It was hard to get out, but I finally said it and he knew what I said. His eyes got so big. I thought he was going to hurt me. Roy finally understands that I know what he is doing. So he stopped. He no longer looks at me with angry or sick eyes. Now all I see is fear and guilt. Roy and I both know that I have something over him now. From this point on, Roy threatens me every chance he gets to make sure I won't tell my family what he has done to me.

If I could just get Lee to stop, I would not say anything to him. I'm scared of him. I understand the difference between sick and crazy. Roy is sick. Lee is crazy. I want so bad to say something or do something to make things better for Momma. I can't stand watching her cry so much, but I don't know what to do or say. I guess all I can do is just stay out of the way and try to sit here and be quiet. It kills me inside when stuff like this happens. I know my brothers Paul and Lamont feel the same way. They get so angry with her boyfriend.

However, she tells them to stay out of her business and that she is going to be OK. But every time he is mean to her, I see Paul and Lamont getting angrier and angrier. I feel that same anger building up inside of me as well. If I'm thinking some of the thoughts that I am thinking, I wonder what Paul and Lamont would like to do to Lee. I also wonder if they get upset with Momma for stopping them from protecting the people they love so much.

My seizures are a way of life for me now. At least two or three times a week, I am going to have them. Coming out of them, I feel so guilty. I know I can't control it, but I wish I could. I feel that I have inconvenienced whoever has to deal with me while the seizures are taking place. The medicine is not preventing them. It is supposed to control them but not prevent them. After skipping a couple of days of taking my seizure medication, I am convinced this is why I feel so weak and tired all the time. I feel like a complete zombie. I try hard to be alert and awake, but there is a feeling that I have to give into when I'm on the medicine. So I have to make the choice of not taking the medication or living every day like a zombie.

One day after I had a really bad seizure, I asked Momma to help me pray. So she led me in these words: "Our Father which art in heaven, hallowed be Thy Name. Thy kingdom come, Thy will be done on earth as it is in heaven. Give us this day our daily bread. And forgive us our debts, as we forgive our debtors. And lead us not into temptation but deliver us from evil. For Thine is the kingdom, and the power, and the glory, forever. Amen."

I know she really believes in those words, even though over the years my absentee father, all of her hard work, and putting up with an abusive boyfriend made her heart bitter. Deep down inside, I know she believes in God, and she raised me to believe in Him. I would like to think all my siblings believe in Christ after Mom worked so hard to make sure we got into church and prayed for us.

By the way, thank God Momma is starting to let go of her grip on me with Paul's help. She has agreed to let me stop taking the seizure medication. She also agreed to let me stop wearing those stupid braces. Momma, the physical therapist, and I all realize that I will never be able to walk and my legs are as strong and straight as they ever will be, so why force me to wear them? They just make me look weird and stand out more. So hallelujah! I don't have to wear those things anymore.

I'm so excited. You have no idea. This speech therapy is paying off for me. I am able to say whatever I am trying to say. I can actually get my words out! Not full sentences, and not everyone understands what I am saying, but my family and teachers are understanding me now more than ever before. It is awesome to be able to communicate with my brothers and sisters. Something else that really gets me excited right now is that I finally realize that the words in my imaginary world are connected to the words I am learning in my speech class, which are connected to the stories my teacher is reading at story time, which are connected to the books that I go into the bathroom and read at night on my own! It's all starting to make sense to me. They are not just made-up words. I am actually learning the things that my brothers and sisters are learning in real school. That excites me so much. Things are getting better. I can't believe it, but things are getting better for me.

I wonder what would happen if they knew all that is going on inside my head. What if everything I am thinking is correct and I just started to say it out loud? Will someone understand my words enough to realize that I am able to read? Should I give it a shot? At this point, what can I lose? Everybody thinks I'm stupid anyway. Tonight, if I get a chance, I am going to try to read out loud to Momma. Let's see if I am right and if she even understands me. But first we all are going to my brothers' basketball game.

There are only two things I hate more than sitting here and watching my brothers run up and down the basketball court. But of those two things, I don't know which one I hate the most: sitting in the cold watching them run up and down the football field or sitting in the heat about to fall asleep as they play the boring game of baseball. I can't play either one of those games. What makes them think I would enjoy watching them? Momma is jumping up and down, hollering at them and trying to tell them what to do next like she is the coach. I just don't get it. By the way, light orange and blue have to be the worst color combination in sports. I can barely look at these two colors when they are standing still. I would get sick if I watched them go up and down the basketball court.

The weather is really bad tonight. It's kind of scary. You can feel the wind shifting our singlewide trailer from side to side. Every now and then, the lights flicker, the sky lights up, and we hear a big boom! It feels and sounds like someone has fired a double-barrel shotgun right beneath our home. I'm sitting in the living room watching TV while waiting for a chance to see if I can truly read or if it is just a part of my imaginary world. In the middle of my cartoon, *Woody the Woodpecker*, the news station interrupts with a loud siren and then begins to scroll words across the screen. Here is my chance; I am going to give it a try. Well, maybe I shouldn't. "WBRZ has issued a tornado warning for the following parishes: Ascension . . ." Who is saying this? The words are coming out of my mouth, but I never gave myself permission to read out loud. They are probably not understanding what I am saying. I should stop.

But Momma and Lamont are walking closer to me as I continue to read. Their eyes are glued to the TV, but their ears are turned toward me. Momma doesn't think I saw her, but she smiled at Lamont while she was listening to me. Every now and then, she pronounced a word that I struggled with. It isn't just a part of my imaginary world; I am putting this together. I can't believe it.

Everything changed after that night. My speech therapy teacher is now trying to get me to say whole words rather than syllables. I am constantly taking different tests during the day at this special school. Momma seems to have a lot more meetings with the principal and teachers. Every day, my teacher is challenging me and believing that I am giving the right answers. The more I speak, the easier it becomes. My brother Lamont believes that I am a genius. He has taken a major interest in my education. He is teaching me more vocabulary words and making me read to him every night before going to bed. I'm not sure that he is even understanding me, but he is listening and responding to me as if he is. It's so great to know that I am not the only one fighting for me to become normal. I am thankful my family, many teachers, and therapists are willing to help me do this. Maybe, just maybe, people will begin to treat me differently now.

That hope didn't last long. Even though I am getting better and can see the changes in my life, it is almost as if it is happening to someone else. I don't think it is really happening to me; it must be happening to someone in my imaginary world. The reason I think this is because people are not seeing what I am feeling. They don't see how much better I am getting. They still treat me as if I was the same baby I was two or three years ago. They even talk to me as if I can't understand anything more than baby talk.

Just the other day, Momma, my two sisters, and myself went into town. While riding down the road, we spotted a car swerving from one lane to the other. Momma was worried that he would cause an accident, so we quickly pulled into the first police station we found. My sisters followed my momma into the building. They must have ran by a man on the way in because he came over to the car to ask me what happened. I was so excited that someone I didn't know had actually asked me a question! But he walked away before I could get two words out. I tried really hard to tell him what was going on, but for some reason, he wasn't willing to listen to me. I'm so angry with myself. I knew what he was asking, but I just couldn't get it out. Why am I locked in this body? Oh well, I'm glad he didn't talk to me anyway. He didn't smell too fresh. He was hot and sweaty, with brown teeth.

Russell, my fourth-to-oldest brother, told us about his day at school. He seems so excited to be sharing what a good day he had. While finishing his story, he looks over at me and says, "I wish you could go to school, Chris." I could not respond without tears. I want so badly to be in school with them. I know I can do it. I know that whatever they are doing, I can do too. I just want to be like them, but for some reason, I'm not given the chance. Everybody who knows me well knows that I am able to learn. It makes me so angry and sad to know that those who do not know me will never give me a chance to prove myself. I don't understand why.

Now I'm in my mom's room, looking into the mirror for the first time. I have seen myself in the mirror, but I never really looked at myself in the mirror. As I look, I can see the difference between me and everyone else. My mouth doesn't move like them. I can't hold my hands like everyone else. No matter how hard I try to sit up straight, my body slowly slumps back into the same position. Now I see what everybody else sees. I am crippled and ugly. I hate what I see in that mirror. No wonder people treat me the way they do. No wonder I'm not allowed to be in school. I understand now why that guy walked away from me. I am hard to look at. I can't hold back the tears. It hurts to be like this. No matter how hard I try not to look deformed, I am, and there's nothing I can do about it. I don't understand why it had to be me.

In my mind, I had the following conversation day after day: "Why don't I feel special? I'm sick of being me. I'm sick of this wheelchair! I'm sick of these legs! I'm sick of people looking at me like I'm some kind of freak or something! I'm sick of sitting alone under a tree day after day! I'm sick of having someone feed me like I'm a baby!"

I'm starting to think no one will accept me for who I am no matter of how much I try. It takes too much time and energy to get to know me, and I am not worth it to most people. I am not really smart. I just got lucky and happened to learn the right pronunciation of these words that I have been reading all these years. The truth is the value of my life will never exceed the value of an animal that is kept locked up as pets and companions. Freedom for me will always be dictated by society.

The Voice of Understanding: Christopher

It didn't matter to Chris if people could understand him at the time. He just wanted to be accepted. He was too young to realize that in order to be accepted, he must first be understood. Someone with no mercy and compassion for a person's situation has not accepted that person. No doubt about that. But on the flip side, people are not perfect. So someone with 100 percent tolerance for another person's situation has not accepted them either. The person that truly accepts them is the one that helps them define their problem without forcing a solution on them. That person is willing to walk in the dark valley, not knowing what is on the other side. Chris wanted the world to accept him based on his strength. I, Christopher, want to be accepted in spite of my weaknesses. Both are necessary for anyone to live a full life in society.

Some people say that I should not let things get me down so easily. They make me feel like I should ignore the way society treats me. My brothers often said to me, "Chris, don't worry about them." That is not possible. Anyone that lives in a society will be affected by that society. Do I have a low self-esteem? Yes, I do. But that low self-esteem was developed over time with the help of society. As hurtful and unhealthy as it may be, we are all easily molded by the people in our lives.

An unmoldable life is a confined life. I had to understand the severity of my disability and feel the pain of that reality. I've come to know that a broken heart is a moldable heart. It was unfortunate that I had to experience a broken heart so early in my life. However, I had to learn that my weaknesses were perfect display cases for my strengths. I didn't know my ability would eventually shine brighter and stronger through my disability.

I have learned that there are traps behind our circumstances. These traps are those subliminal messages that we allow to penetrate our minds and invoke fear and failure in our hearts. After years of being defined by society, Chris is finding himself in the midst of these traps. It is not my disability that makes me disabled; it is society's response to my disability that debilitates me. Chris was at a point where he let society convince him that his physical condition defined his mental capability. He didn't understand that there was no way around rejection. Therefore, he allowed society to trap him. In time, he will learn that there is a moment between stepping into a trap and the moment that trap is set. In those spilt seconds, you can actually break free. Something in me constantly waited for those moments. I know what it feels like to be trapped. The feeling of being confined creates a deep desire to escape.

Eventually, I was too old for the special school I attended. From there, I went to an elementary school that had a special program for kids with disabilities. We spent all day in one room coloring and watching movies. Some of the kids were able to go to art class with all the other kids. But, basically, we were all in the same room. The testing and evaluation did not stop. I continued to be pulled aside by visitors of the school. They were trying to figure out just how much I knew. I just continued to answer the questions to the best of my ability and study at home with Lamont.

I didn't know how much progress I was going to experience over the years. Here is what I know now: I have gotten this far, so why not keep going? Sometimes our goal in life can be the bars around our true potential. Believe it or not, a goal can confine a person. A person can reach a point in their life where their goal is accomplished and they no longer strive to do more. They say to themselves, "I have accomplished this. Therefore, I am successful." But success for an individual doesn't come until he has exhausted his potential. One can exhaust their potential vocationally and still not reach success. It is not until the individual has exhausted their potential—personal, physical, spiritual, professional, or financial—that they find success in their life. With that in mind, I can boldly say that I am not the only one that has confined potential. I can't prove it, but I do believe that every one of us has not truly reached success according to this definition.

I told the Head Special Ed teacher that I was going to college. She told me that wasn't in the plan for me. At best, I would stay in this special program until eighteen or nineteen. Then maybe if I'm lucky, I could go to a special trade school and learn a trade that someone would hire me to do. But for some reason, that negativity did not faze me this time. I knew my potential did not stop there. At that point in my life, I knew that I was going to achieve more than anyone expected. I had no doubt that one day I would attend college, even though I did not know how it was going to happen. Yes, this was a lofty goal, but it was also a goal that allowed me to expand and grow.

Our perception decides if truth is going to be our captor or our liberator. Sometimes we think just because one person won't give us the opportunity to be who we are, no one else will either. I realized that Chris set the trap of rejection. He is the one that rejected us before anyone else did. He is not giving us a chance to see if the other person will give us a chance. This mind-set prevents us from being rejected but is actually denying us the possibility of being accepted. For a long time, Chris just sat down in that trap. He rejected us before anyone else had the opportunity to do it for him. My disability, my attitude, and my passion for life are what the world needed to see in order to accept me. I believe deep down inside, if I live my life honestly and let people see my weaknesses as well as my strengths, I will ultimately change everyone's outlook about a person with a disability.

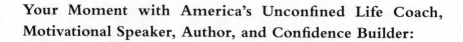

Your Moment with America's Unconfined Life Coach, Motivational Speaker, Author, and Confidence Builder:

We all have refining moments in life. Our ability to see the truth decides if that moment is an opportunity or a trap.

Are you hoping to be accepted by people who cannot understand you?
How has society affected your life?
Are you standing in a trap, giving it time to confine you?

CHAPTER 9

People Change

The Voice of Experience: Chris

A lot has changed over the years. As far as school, I spend more time being pulled aside to take test than I do attending class with the rest of the students. My homework has changed too. I guess I knew eventually it would happen. Mom paid off the trailer and bought a house. My older brothers stayed in the trailer and are paying the utilities. I guess I knew deep down inside my brothers and sisters would eventually have their own lives, but the truth is it never really sunk in until now. I thought we would always be a tight, close-knit family living under the same roof. It is so hard for me to get used to this. My life has gone from having four older brothers that completely took care of me and supported me in everything to having no brothers living with me at all. This is very hard.

On top of the change of not living under the same roof, we are all so different. The effects of growing up in this community have shaped and molded each one of our personalities differently. Everyone takes life in their own way; therefore, the outcome is different for each individual. This is so true in my family.

My sisters and I did not get along for a long time. There were times when they were not sensitive to my physical condition, like any other kid at that age. They too made fun of me by teasing me with something they could do and I couldn't. Or they would not give me something I needed until my brothers or mother would make them give it to me.

Christina and I joke around all the time. She says all the time, "I am the Beauty. He is the Beast." To which I say, "Yep, she has the looks, but I have the brains."

Christina and I share a similar passion in life. We both want peace, family, friends, and to feel loved. For us, material things are nice but secondary. At the end of the day, we both want to feel like we belong. We are very social and outgoing. When we are not competing with each other, we are a dynamic team and could easily be the life of the party. Where Christina and I are different is in how far we would go for that peace. She wakes up every day of her life with priorities. Anything or anyone that are not a part of those priorities is pushed aside. The severity of the issue does not matter. She is only going to do what she deems important that day. Therefore, the people around her can feel insignificant. However, we are closer than we have ever been before because we are the only two in the house now. Even though she is going into ninth grade and she has her own friends, we still hang out at home and talk a lot.

If I believe that people are a product of their environment, Angela would be the perfect example. Of all seven of us, she struggles the most with our financial condition as well as the absenteeism of our father. Her desire to be Daddy's little princess has not been met. Therefore, she forces everyone else to treat her as if she's a princess. This makes it a challenge to get along with her. Showering her with attention for the first two years as the only girl may have also laid the foundation for her need for attention now. Meaning, she knows the world doesn't revolve around her but believes it should. She will definitely help someone that is in dire need, but only if there is no one else there to do it. She will always put herself before the needs of others. I believe it is natural for people who are brought up in a tough economic condition to desire more for their life, but Angela takes it a bit farther than most, in my opinion.

Angela's dream to be a supermodel is not going to happen. She is cute and definitely has the body for it: tall and slim. However, in these days, if you are not a light-skinned black girl, you don't make the cut. I know this makes her bitter. Angela and I can get along OK if I don't challenge her, which I always do. In her mind, she is never wrong. If there is anyone I would fight with in the family, it is Angela. Yep, you know it, oil and water. She is off in New Jersey living with the family of some boy that she fell in love with. We don't hear from her much, but I have a feeling she will be back soon.

Russell and Dewayne both have been doing their own thing for a long, long time now. I hear Momma talking about them, and I know that she is afraid to fully release them into the community we live in. She always said," There is too much out there that you don't understand yet." They also each have a child out of wedlock already.

Just like all my other brothers, Russell had no problem taking care of me when Mom wasn't around. Every now and then, he will fuss at me if I don't do something right that he knows I can do. He is the only one out of my brothers that disciplines me. Russell is madly in love with this girl from Baton Rouge. I am sure he will be married to her real soon.

There is a professional wrestler called "the Junk Yard Dog." That is also my brother Russell's nickname. Like "The Dog," Russell is well-built, very black, athletic, strong, bold, not to be taken lightly, but polite. Everyone who meets him loves him. You can count on him. He may complain about it, but he is always going to do what he says he will do. Pleasant is the appropriate word to describe him, pleasant to a fault, that is. There is a big concern now with Russell. He has a tendency to lie and scheme to get whatever he wants.

Dewayne is someone who dances to his beat and his beat alone. At the age of sixteen, he moved out of my mom's house and into my grandmother's house because she had no problem letting him do what he wanted to do. Now keep in mind that my grandmother's house was less than a half a football field from our home.

Dewayne holds a special place in my heart because of his hot temper. I remember one weekend, when everyone was invited over for a swimming party except for me, for whatever reason. Because I was not invited, Dewayne turned down the opportunity and borrowed my cousin's car to make up for it. We went to the mall and had the best time. He was determined to make those two days a fun time for me.

Dewayne is still the type that if he wants to do something for you, it is still going to be when he wants to do it, what he wants to do, and how he wants to do it. If he doesn't want to do it, there is no way he is going to do it. He is by far the smartest one in the bunch. He is also a hard worker. He has a good job and bought his first brand-new car, and things are looking good for him. But we are sure his talent will eventually go to waste. The community is eating him alive and sucking him dry.

The only way to see the other side of Lamont come out is to provoke him. Paul is very good at that! Lamont is definitely not a go-getter. Yet I would say that out of all my siblings, he is the one who is truly reaching his full potential. From high school, he went straight into a manual labor job and married his high school sweetheart. However, it seems that he doesn't have much time for us anymore. I most of all miss having him around. Lamont was in and out of trouble a little bit but it didn't last long. He just can't take the disappointment of the people around him.

Paul has the ability to bounce back at any time, no matter what he is going through. When he wants to be, he can become the male version of our mom, strong willed and determined to succeed. As soon as he could, Paul got a job at Payless, the local food store, while going to high school and playing football. Though he loved sports, they weren't enough to keep him in school. As soon as he was seventeen, he quit high school and started working full time.

Even now, Paul makes sure I have whatever I need or want at all times, if it is in his control. He spoils me rotten! He is also my mouthpiece when it comes to me doing something that seems difficult or even dangerous to my mom. In anyone's life, especially someone with a severe disability, it is very hard to find someone that totally believes in your ability to achieve and conquer. Paul is that person for me. I will never have another person that believes in me as much as he does. In my life, Paul is definitely a tool in God's hands.

In this community there are a lot of single moms raising large families. In most of these families the older siblings are forced to take the role of helping their mother in raising the rest of the children; both financially and parentally. This caused the older sibling to grow up quickly and make choices that may damage their future. Paul was no different. His choices are beginning to get him into trouble. Mom makes it known that this is not acceptable, but the trait we all got from her is stubbornness. Paul thinks this is the solution for our financial problem, and no one can tell him it isn't. That choice is eating him up, it's no longer just a way to help momma, it's becoming his identity. This funny, warm-hearted, giving big brother of mine, who supports me in everything, is now slowly destroying his life.

Watching your hero destroy his life is internal torture. It is like watching Superman living for the next time he could get his hands on kryptonite. It seems like the very thing that is killing him is the one thing he wants most in life. This life blinds him to the fact that this life is destroying him and hurting everyone around him. It is not only painful for me to watch him do this to himself; I also have to watch him throw away the life I am working so hard to have. It almost seems like Paul is disregarding the struggle and challenges I face every day. I'm convinced that if he could feel the pain he is causing me, he would change.

One of the hardest things for me to understand is why people choose to use drugs and alcohol as an escape from their problems. I understand that life is hard, and I know what it feels like to have to get up and fight for something. I had to fight to learn how to pick up a spoon. I had to fight to learn how to sit up halfway straight in a chair! I had to fight just to learn how to open my own mouth to talk! I will have to fight the rest of my life just to be accepted. If I can get out of my bed every day and just think about going out there to face the world without looking for an escape, then why can't others do the same?

Momma is known in the white community as a hard worker. For the last five years, she has held down three jobs, working day in and day out to take care of us. Her philosophy is excellence. When it comes to her work, she does everything to the best of her abilities. She is the first person her employers call on when they need something done.

I always knew Momma was a fireball, but now I am starting to realize she is much more than that. Momma is a fighter to the core. In the black community, Momma is known as someone you want to keep your distance from. She might not be as quick to fight for herself, but when it comes to her kids, she will literally kill someone. She has been known to take on anyone, including her own brothers. She is also one who takes the law into her own hands. If you are wrong in her eyes, she will hold you accountable, whether you are an outsider or a member of her own family. This has gotten her into trouble a couple of times, but she would say it was worth it.

Momma is giving Lee, her boyfriend, a run for his money. All of a sudden, he is getting to know the Gladys that the rest of our community knows, the Gladys who would slap the crap out of you at any point in time, the Gladys who would cuss you out so bad that you would feel like crap for even waking up that morning. Just the other day, she and Lee got into an argument. He tried to leave. Just as he stepped out of the bedroom door, I heard my momma's hand slap him on the back, then the collar of his shirt tightened against his neck, and she jerked him back into the room right before the door slammed. All I heard then was, "Gladys, get your crazy ass away from me!" I'm loving it. It's about time she defended herself. He may have torn her down, but he definitely can't hold her down. I don't think it will be long before the relationship comes to a screeching halt.

I remember a couple of years ago when my cousin had a graduation party at the fairground across the street from where we lived. Some boys came over from the other side of the tracks, if you will, to start some trouble. My mom found out about this and knew that my brothers and cousins were outnumbered, and this group of guys had guns and knives. Now remember that I said she would kill for her kids, so this did not go over well with her. She quickly jumped in the car and within ten minutes was back with a whole cavalry of friends and relatives ready to defend the family and our territory.

My brothers Paul, Lamont, Dewayne, and Russell are natural fighters. But there was something different in their attitudes when they knew that Momma was right there fighting with them. To sum it all up, my family is known as a family you don't want to fight with. You especially don't want to make Gladys Coleman mad. Everyone knows that.

Momma may not be the perfect mother, but I will never take for granted her dedication to motherhood. I know she works hard to give us the home that we have. Now I realize that working three jobs and raising seven kids had to have taken a toll on her. So many times I watched her come home, cook, clean, and go right back out the door to her next job. I have never seen her cry about the responsibility of raising all seven of us by herself. There are times I can remember her praying beside her bed every night. I didn't realize that was a response to God that our culture has forgotten about. Yes, we pray to God, but very few of us get down on our knees at night and pray with our heads bowed. I remember her saying one night, "Only You can fix this, God."

━━━►·◆·◄━━━

Your Moment with America's Unconfined Life Coach, Motivational Speaker, Author, and Confidence Builder:

"Can people change?" is a ridiculous question. Everyone changes at some point in their life. Many times, the people we wish would change have changed. They may have seen a need to become the person you want to change now. The right questions may be "Do they see a need to make a change? Or why are they choosing to remain the same?"

Are you waiting for, fighting, embracing, or demanding a change?
Do you give the people around you space and time to deal with life in their own way?
Do you want people in your life to change for their good or just to line up with your expectations?

CHAPTER 10

Education Is an Opportunity

The Voice of Experience: Chris

All of the testing and evaluation over the past couple of years have stopped at last. I feel like I have been used as an academic test rat. Some of the test administrators were trying to prove my intelligence, while others were trying to disprove it. How do I know this? There were many that gave me a smile and a word of encouragement every time I answered a question right. However, there were also many that looked at me in disbelief and asked me the same questions in different fashions, trying to trip me up or make me doubt my answers. Nevertheless, the results are in. Everything that has been going on inside my head for all these years wasn't just a fantasy. They were reality, and somehow I have managed to give myself a ninth-grade education.

It's official; I am going to high school. I'll only be two years behind my twin sister Christina. Originally, they were going to keep me in the resource room all day and teach me what the regular kids were learning in their individual classes, but Christina asked them why. She told them that I was smarter than she was, and if she can handle going to class, so can I. I am so excited. I am finally getting a chance to show the world who I am. I have a chance to show everyone that there is more to me than this body.

At first, Momma wasn't too keen on the possibility of me going into high school. I think she didn't want to set me up for failure. She believed that it would be too much for me to deal with. But my brother Paul knew that this was something I desperately wanted, so he convinced her to help me get there.

The hardest part of growing up disabled is dealing with rejection. A disability is automatically looked at as a negative physical characteristic to have. As a result, you are bound to face rejection. For me, it is rejection from my father as well as from the outside world, especially in school. It is very hard to go down the hallway of my school and know that not one person wants to be friends with me. High school is the one place outside of my home that I know I belong in. However, the other kids do not embrace me at all. They have absolutely no desire to get to know me.

They are constantly making fun of my speech, imitating the way my arms and legs move, and laughing at me every chance they get. There is this one boy who loves to hit my hand while I am trying to drive my electric wheelchair, causing me to run into the walls so everybody could laugh at me. Today, he took it too far. I didn't run into a wall; I ran into our biology teacher, right there in the middle of the hallway. This tall teacher fell down, dropping all of her papers all over the place. Everybody in the hall busted out laughing while hiding their faces and trying to pretend that the chuckles were not coming from them. I know this is going to be the talk of the school all week. I am so embarrassed because it looks like I ran into her on purpose. I think she is going to be mad at me and make her class especially difficult for me.

I never thought I would experience it, but I was actually called a "nigger" today. Not just a "nigger" but a "crippled f—ing nigger." I have heard about prejudiced white people before from my mom and my brothers and sisters, but I never thought I would experience it.

After all, the majority of the people who helped me get here were white teachers and therapists. They never seemed to have any issues with me, but now I realize that I am living down South in Louisiana where bigotry is still a large part of society. It is still a social no-no if you are dating someone or have a good friend outside of your race. Mom and my brothers and sisters all have white friends, but my family and their friends are not very well accepted in their own race because of their inter-racial friendships. I knew racism was real, but now I am starting to experience the reality and gravity of it. Now I understand that I am rejected by society because of my disability, but I am also hated by a larger part of society because of my color. And when these two overlap, life becomes very difficult for me.

Students are not the only ones making it difficult for me. There is a teacher who decided she is not going to pay any attention to me while I am in her class. She told me her class was not a daycare. I have to admit this really bothers me. After all these years of fighting to get here, I can't believe a teacher would deny me this opportunity. But I am going to change her opinion of me. I have learned that respect is something you have to earn. Because I have a disability, that respect requires me to work a lot harder than the average person. People expect less out of me, so it's my responsibility to give them more.

I thought I would have a refuge in Momma's arms. For so many years, she did a wonderful job at making me feel safe, secure, and loved. I remember many nights she would come in late from work and pray for me, hold me, and simply give me a kiss and then walk back out the door. Not anymore. After fighting so hard to get me *into* high school, she made it very clear that she would not help me get *through* high school. I know it sounds ironic, but she told me, "If you want this, you have to do it yourself." That meant that I had to wake myself up in the morning and get fully dressed on my own. Mom would fix breakfast, but I was in charge of everything else I needed to do in order to get to the bus on time. However, parents have eyes in the back of their heads, as they say, so from her bed, she listens to every move I make and at least twice every morning points out something that she doesn't think I am doing right, even though she is not in the bedroom or bathroom with me. After school, it is my responsibility to get myself in the house, get my work done, and get ready for the next morning. This may seem hard to some people, but I am actually glad. It feels like Momma was off my back in some ways and allowing me the chance to become my own person.

Fortunately for me, I have six brothers and sisters that have already graduated from this high school. Their reputations weren't for their academic abilities. Nevertheless, they have gained much respect here. Paul, Darrell, Dewayne, and Russell were known for their athletic abilities and have brought many trophies home over the years. Christina and Angela were both two very popular girls. They both played basketball, and Christina was actually on the homecoming court. Once everyone figured out that I was the last Coleman, things began to change. Some students feared having my brothers and sisters come at them because of something they did to me, while the teachers were eager to have another Coleman in their class because of our well-behaved manners. My siblings and I always feared what Mom would do to us if we ever cut up in school. Teachers also know that Mrs. Coleman is the last person they want to see come on campus. Mom has been known for setting a few teachers, administrators, students, and their parents straight. Therefore, there is quite a reputation that comes with the Coleman name, and I am going to use that to my advantage.

By the time the second semester of my freshman year rolled around, the teachers and guidance counselors decided that I still wasn't given the opportunity to live up to my academic potential. They changed my classes from a simple graduating track to college prep courses. That next year, I was enlisted in AP (advanced placement) biology, chemistry, history, and algebra. The tables were truly turning. Teachers were excited about the possibility of me going to college and were willing to help me get there.

I spend the last hour of every day in the resource room. A lot of other students and I come here periodically during the day. Most of them come because they need help understanding the material that the teachers are going through in the regular class. I mostly come to catch up with my homework or take a test. It takes a lot longer for me to get my answers on paper than other students, so they allow me to bring it back to the resource class. We have at least three or four teachers every hour in this class; they all support and encourage me. I feel like they are impressed with my academic ability, and they desperately want to see me achieve. I am the class clown. I have a good relationship with all the teachers, so I can cut up, and they really seem to love it. I really didn't know that this was a part of my personality, but when I am with them, I feel like it is OK to lighten up.

I am in my third year of high school now. I'm loving it. There was a lot I didn't know, but I knew a lot of the material from the books I read prior to going to high school. This made it easy for me to keep up with the teachers. I remember the first time I solved a math problem in class. I knew I could do the algebra problem, hands down. I had no doubt I could tell the teacher letter by letter, number by number, and symbol by symbol, how to solve that equation. I wanted to answer so badly, but I believed I shouldn't because of the possibility of no one understanding me and getting it wrong. Before I knew it, my hand was up in the air, and the teacher called on me. My heart was beating inside of my chest so hard and fast, I could actually hear it. There was a big lump in my throat, but I actually gave her the answer. I can't believe I did that! She wrote every number and letter that came out of my mouth onto the board. Every time I got a piece of the equation right, she said, "Mmhm mmhm," which only gave me more confidence and made me want to go further. Out of the corner of my eye, I even caught a slight smile by one of my peers, so I knew I was doing it right. I finally wrapped it up and gave the complete answer. The teacher looked at me with a big grin on her face. Another student on the other side of the room was shaking his head and smiling at me. Then everyone in the room broke out into quiet chatter among themselves. They were surprised. This is it! This is how I get people to like me and take me seriously. All I have to do is impress them with my knowledge. I can do this. My education is the key to my cage.

The school system thinks they are doing me a favor by giving me a chance to go to high school. I see it as more than a chance. It is an opportunity. It is the key to the cage I feel locked into. People can think I am "retarded" all they want, but if they slip up and give me a moment, I will show them that I am just as intelligent as they are, if not more so. I will turn the tables on them. I don't know where this mind-set came from. I never had a thought that confident in my whole life!

I think the best way to get people to accept me is to impress them and live up to their standards. Every time I am out of my home, I find myself trying to impress someone, trying to show them that I am capable and knowledgeable.

By my junior year, my high school experience dramatically changed. I would say that I was one of the most popular guys in the student body. The best part of my day was rolling into the lunchroom and having an instant crowd around me. I felt like I belonged there. I was one of the guys. Just based on my popularity, I was able to win my campaign for treasurer of the senior class. Our mascot was an alligator; therefore, my campaign slogan was "Vote for the Rolling Gator." And they did.

I have been going to church a lot with my mom. Before now, it was just something we did. Going to church has always been a part of our lives. I read the Bible one time when I was secretly reading books in the bathroom. I didn't understand it all. All the thee's and thou's, etc. But it had some interesting stories in there. I also enjoy listening to our pastor elaborate on the stories. I don't quite know where he gets all that he is pulling out of it, but it sounds like some good principles to live by.

One lady in the church has taken a special interest in me, which is ironic because she is also in the education system and was one of the ones that were trying to disprove my academic abilities. But now that the word is out that I am very intelligent, will likely be going to college, and do more than anyone dreamed that I would be able to do, she wants to be a part of my success story. I know she has a motive behind what she is doing for me, but I am getting to go to church more often so I am just using her the same way she is using me.

Church is going good. Besides that, when I look at how far I have come, I believe that God has His hands on me. I went straight from being in a special class for the mentally disabled to taking college prep classes. It doesn't take too much for me to believe that there is a God in heaven who is in control of my situation and is working everything out.

I was starting to resonate with this, but then one night, someone said something to make me pull back from the drawing I felt to God. One Wednesday night in Bible study, someone told me that the reason that I wasn't healed was because I did not have the faith to be. I didn't believe in God enough to be healed. What does that mean? You either believe in Him or you don't. Why isn't everyone disabled until they have enough faith in Christ? Why is He using me as His faith guinea pig? That night, my warm heart went back to cold. Now I am putting all of my efforts and attention into my education.

In school, I spent too much time wanting to change people's opinions of a person with a disability, rather than just simply taking the opportunity that I had been given. A person that is too busy fighting a change rather than recognizing the opportunity to turn the tables and break free is living a confined life. There are moments in our lives when a door opens or a window is cracked. At that time, the grip of the situation is weakened and becomes vulnerable, giving us the perfect opportunity to escape. When this opportunity presents itself, many of us are preoccupied with questions like, "Why is this window cracked? What took so long for this door to open?"

Opportunities of freedom are passed up and overlooked because we have embraced a slavery mentality. Meaning, we think that beyond the open door and cracked window, there is our master waiting to penalize us and shove us back into the corner. This assumption stops us from taking steps toward the opportunity that has been given to us. We find ourselves living for a change that will create an opportunity, rather than taking the opportunity to make a change.

Your Moment with America's Unconfined Life Coach, Motivational Speaker, Author, and Confidence Builder:

Some people turn down opportunity for the sake of their family. They believe that to have the family's name, they must deny the opportunity to become their own person. Yes, it is a fine line between becoming your own person and living off your family's reputation. To walk that fine line, you must create for yourself opportunities while carrying the family's torch.

Based on who you are, how can you create opportunities for yourself? Are you taking the opportunity to make your dreams your reality? Do you have someone in your life pushing you to go further than your family's name?

CHAPTER 11

Understanding Limitations

The Voice of Understanding: Christopher

Chris didn't want Mom to deal with the reality of what Roy was doing because he felt like she had been through enough. Today as the man Christopher, I am afraid of how my friends will see me. There is a lot of shame, anger, and humiliation in this confession; but I have to get it out, what Roy did was wrong and it damaged my life. This has to be said because the incident has and it continues to play a significant role in my life.

Unfortunately, my situation is not unique. A large percentage of people with disabilities experience physical and/or sexual abuse. This issue is not brought to light because of a lack of acknowledgment and exposure. Society does not want to go there. The thought of someone preying on the disabled is something we are not ready to come to terms with. But here are the facts:

- Fifteen percent of children who are sexually abused have a disability (National Center on Child abuse and Neglect).

- More than 90 percent of people with developmental disabilities will experience sexual abuse at some time in their lives (JP Das Developmental Disabilities Centre).
- Forty-nine percent will experience ten or more abusive incidents (JP Das Developmental Disabilities Centre).

Not to mention individuals with disabilities remain today a devalued population. Therefore, there is not enough social awareness for this injustice to be brought to the surface and dealt with. Hopefully, my story will change that.

My vision will always be subdued by the knowledge or lack of knowledge of those around me. However, this fact did not stop me from taking on the same hopes and dreams as any other kid. I wanted to make my fantasy world into my reality. It was all just a matter of hard work and persistence, so I thought.

The reality was, and still is, everything people do without thinking is something that I have to carefully plan in order for me to undertake that task and conserve energy. Every day of my life has been and continues to be a constant battle that I will never be able to win without physical pain and exhaustion. Jerking and shaking is a twenty-four-hour activity for me. I remember the first time I tried to feed myself. I wrapped my fingers around the spoon and lifted it. Just as I reached my mouth, my hand quickly took a U-turn. All of the food ended up on my lap. Even today, I eat very few things with a fork because of the fear of stabbing myself in the lip, tongue, or teeth. When it comes to eating, it takes 90–100 percent concentration with absolutely no distractions whatsoever. I don't even try to drink out of a glass. I simply use a straw. Eating, dressing myself, brushing my teeth, or something as simple as turning on the TV with the remote will always be a difficult task.

Even now, it is embarrassing when my muscles cause me to lose control in front of my friends. A lot of times they laugh, and I laugh with them. But reality is I'm ashamed that it has happened. I feel like

I draw attention to myself and inconvenience everyone around me. This makes me feel like I do not fit in with the rest of the crowd.

Chris continued to struggle with the fact that he had to crawl around on the floor to get from room to room in his home. My sisters even picked up on this insecurity I had when we got older. They often used it to get back at me when we're in an argument by saying, "You crawl around on all fours like a dog." Oftentimes I tried to turn it around on them when their friends came over. I was aware that their friends were fearful of me because I was crawling around on all fours, as well as the evidence in my appearance that I had problem controlling my fine motor skills. So I would use this to scare them away by barking at them when they came around. I thought for a long time Chris did this mostly to get back at them, but now I realize it was how I felt about myself.

There have been many times that I ask myself *Why*, especially as a young boy. That question cannot be avoided when you live with a disability. I had a low self-esteem, and out of my pain, I embrace that self-esteem. The way I dealt with my siblings' friends, along with other people who made it very obvious they were uncomfortable with me, was a cover-up for what I felt about myself. I intentionally made them even more uncomfortable. I thought it would be better to give them what they expected instead of showing them what they did not expect.

You may ask when I stopped asking the question, "Why?" The truth is I have never stopped asking. Even today I am still asking the question, but in a different sentence structure. I've gone from "Why me?" to "What is your purpose?" to "What is your will?" I have to say that I have come a long way to get to that training of thought.

There were a few things I did not understand yet. One, my disability always will play a role in my life. That role will either complicate or enhance my accomplishments. Second, in spite of my abilities, society will always limit me based on my disability. I will spend more energy proving to society I can do a task than actually doing a task. And, finally, the people who are closest to me will always have subconscious perceptions of a person with a disability. Society has limited their view on my situation as well. I had to accept the physical limitations of my disability and at the same time fight against society's stigma of people with disabilities. I needed to draw a line between accepting my physical limitations and allowing society's preconceived limitations to dictate my life.

I have learned people are not trapped in circumstances. They are trapped in their mind-sets about their circumstances. Individuals often remain confined because they are afraid of the consequences and the responsibility of being free. It wasn't my disability that kept me reliant on my wheelchair. It was the power of the disabled label and the opinions of a dysfunctional society that confined me. The reason why Chris lived so much of his life confined is because he denied who he was and was not doing the things he needed to do to move on. The only way I would continue to live my life trapped in my circumstances is if I allowed Chris to exist in an atmosphere of denial. Complacency is something that every one of us has to confront at some point of our lives. In order to obtain real freedom we must put forth effort, be diligent, and continue to have a positive attitude about our situation. The secret of getting out of whatever it is that confines us is to simply get over ourselves. No doubt about it, Chris had a mountain to climb.

I have realized that purpose is not complicated; it's simply momentary. Every moment we are allowed to live is because our lives have a purpose for that moment. Whatever the purpose, it never requires more than what a person has at that point in their life. I did not understand that letting someone see me smile in my condition and hear me say thank you in my circumstances was the purpose behind my life. I have made a difference just by living with joy. I didn't know then as I know now that in my worst state of being, purpose can be found.

All I knew at the time was that my life was going to be difficult because of my disability. I didn't know that joy and victory were waiting for me under my circumstances. I did not realize I had to go through the circumstances to find peace with who I am rather than trying to escape from my reality. I had to learn how to allow my life to be a tool God could use. I really believe my family and closest friends are motivated, challenged, and encouraged by me by just being who I am. Chris, the boy I was, didn't know it; but one day, through his life, he will get the opportunity to help people press beyond boundaries in all areas of their lives. But it has been said before, to whom much is given, much is expected. Over the course of the next few years, I will go through the hard lesson of learning that this disability is not a curse but a gift.

Your Moment with America's Unconfined Life Coach, Motivational Speaker, Author, and Confidence Builder:

We have within us the ability to change our curses into blessings. That ability is utilized when we decide to live out our purpose.

What is your purpose for this time in your life?
Do you have the courage to come out of the corner of life?
What would it take to change your reality?

CHAPTER 12

Diamond in the Rough

The Voice of Understanding: Christopher

Having the key of education in my hand made Chris a show-off. He so desperately wanted to be accepted and loved impressing people so much that he took it overboard. He developed a cocky and matter-of-fact attitude. That was his way of protecting himself from further rejection. Or is it really a weakness that I, Christopher, have that was coming out through Chris? This may be good for Chris' self-esteem, but for me, it may be something that I need to be cautious of. I said to myself, "They can point out everything I can't do physically, but they cannot deny my intellect." It took a long time for me to realize this, but success can be just as confining as failure. Failure took on a whole new meaning for me. Even now to this day, failure doesn't mean I made a mistake; it means, to me, I am not sufficient because of my disability. The pressure of trying to impress someone every day, around the clock, has taken a toll on me.

For the next five to six years, Chris and I joined the same team in the game "fake it till you make it." The point of the game is to do whatever it takes to survive until you achieve what you want to achieve. I watched my mom play this game for many years in order to raise seven kids on her own. It would be safe to say that I was trained by one of the pros. Some of the teachers and principals saw me more as a project rather than a student who had a lot of potential. I was an opportunity for them to receive recognition and advancement in their careers. So when school officials from the school board came around to evaluate what was going on, I smiled and answered as many questions as I could, while pretending to sing that teacher's praises. However, my focus was getting to college. If I had to allow myself to be their token student, then so be it.

I also allowed several of the students to continue bullying me. They did everything from calling me "crippled" and a "nigger," to breaking my wheelchair, to ramming me into walls whenever they could. I knew that speaking up and telling the administrators about it would only cause more problems. Telling my mom or my brothers would have probably gotten me kicked out of school because they would have definitely come to my defense. I worked too hard to get here to allow this to happen. So once again when people treated me unfairly, I gritted my teeth and kept quiet. I did not understand that this was becoming a pattern in my life.

I thought to myself, no one wanted to hear the hardships I experienced as a child. Some would not even recognize that it happened. It would only further complicate my life and make it more difficult for me to achieve the things that I wanted to achieve. So I told myself it did not happen. "It was just a part of my imaginary world." I shoved the pain, anger, and disappointment I had deep down in my gut; and I went on with my life. I had no intention of ever letting the abuse, pain, and rejection to ever come back to the surface.

Chris hasn't admitted it yet, but the fact my father doesn't want anything to do with me weighs heavily on my heart. He comes around every once in a while and says, "Hi." Then he disappears for four or five months at a time. I can't help but be cold toward him. My family thinks that it doesn't bother me. I make comments like "That's not my father. I don't have a father" or "Paul is the only father

I know" and shrug it off as if it doesn't matter to me. But deep down inside, it does. It's just another thing I have to fake until I make it.

We have a tendency to tell ourselves a lie in order to survive. We want to say it's not a lie; it's just our way of coping with the situation. In order to just cope with a situation, there has to be some amount of deceit. I felt the need to protect and preserve all the things I was able to accomplish thus far. I did not realize there was a fine line between tolerating something and being comfortable where you are. The fact of the matter is I spent the next five years tolerating people and issues because I knew bringing the issues to the table would be uncomfortable for some and therefore unbearable for me.

I have found that the worst thing someone can do to themselves is to try to live up to a definition of success defined by society. Society will tell you success is the car you drive, the position you hold, and the caliber of people you hang around. If you can't impress someone by those three elements, then you are unsuccessful. I have learned the hard way that this is not the truth. For me, success is the outcome of my sacrifices. Anyone who wants to accomplish much must also sacrifice much. They have to grow into their full potential.

No wonder I don't fit in. The stigma of a disabled label totally contradicts the meaning of success in their eyes. Labeling people is not helping society; it is hindering society. This activity is making individuals too insecure to bring their God-given gifts and abilities to the table. Therefore, we are taking the chance of delaying or possibly never discovering the solution to problems in this world. We believe that the solution has to come from an individual who operates at maximum performance; but oftentimes, if we open our minds, we will find that the solution lies within the guy who lives in a wheelchair or with autism.

Another thing I have observed that we live in a society that expects me to be ashamed of my family. They label me as "disabled" and my family as "dysfunctional." For now I want to talk to you about what some might call my "dysfunctional" family.

First and foremost, I am not ashamed of them. They are the vessels that God has used to shape and mold Chris into Christopher. The world often calls the perfect family the one with a father in the home, a mother, two kids, a dog, and a white picket fence. This family will present itself as perfect. They own a big house and a nice car, and the world will see no fault in their Sunday morning presentation. I will petition to you that *this* could very well be the dysfunctional family. If someone were a fly on the wall in this so-called perfect home, they would probably see things they never thought would be in the midst of this family. This family does not want others to see their imperfection. Yet these are the individuals we allow to represent our society and define other people as dysfunctional.

No doubt about it, I am part of a rough family. The community is that of violence, drugs, alcohol, and a survival mentality. This rough environment was the catalyst for me to one day shine. That's right. I am a diamond in the rough.

Now you may wonder how I am going to shine after growing up in an environment like that. What is my view of life? How has my family shaped me into who I am? I too had my pitfalls, stumbling blocks, and demons along the way. It just didn't look the same as the rest of my family. But at the end of the day, the ultimate judge will see beneath the surface of everyone and hold us each accountable according to our sins, including me. Let's just say I see myself in every one of my family members, and though we are a lot alike, I also think my life is turning out to be very different from theirs. I see things from a different perspective because of my disability. That perspective forced me to make different decisions, and those decisions produced a different outcome.

Our decisions have power over us. Decisions plus results always equals consequences in our lives. Our decisions and the results of those decisions are the cornerstones of where we are today. We end up at certain points in our lives because of the decisions we have made. I made the decision to reach my potential in spite of my surroundings.

A person who is allowing his surroundings to be boundaries around his potential is living a confined life. Every individual is the core of his atmosphere. Their atmosphere is made up of layers that many times need to be carved away to find their true potential. Our family's perspective on life is the first and closest layer around our core. The collective mentality of the environment around us is the next layer. Then we have the stereotypes that society places on us because of our immediate environment. These layers do not destroy one's potential; they simply hide them. The individual has the responsibility to pull back the layers and expose his or her true potential.

Peeling an apple is not about reaching the core as much as it is about exposing the core. The core of an apple is the only thing that is not eaten up. The person who is not eaten up by life is the one who focuses on his potential rather than his surroundings. I know there is something in me that has to find a way out. I have to show it to the rest of the world. I believe when the layers of my hard life are peeled back, and my core is exposed something great will be discovered.

Your Moment with America's Unconfined Life Coach, Motivational Speaker, Author, and Confidence Builder:

Life wasn't meant to be an eighty-year masquerade party. People and situations make us think that we have to cover up and pretend to be someone we're not. A diamond in the rough is rare and therefore precious to many. You will not only add value to your life but to those around you as well when you expose who you truly are.

When will you become tired of faking it until you make it?
Are you afraid of exposing your core and therefore will not peel back the layers in your life?
Have you defined success and failure for yourself?

CHAPTER 13

Chris to Christ

The Voice of Experience: Chris

A couple of months ago, there was a big picture of me in the *Advocate*, a Baton Rouge newspaper. Here are some of the things they said in the article:

> Chris Coleman was born a prisoner but after years of chipping at the mortar, the walls of his prison are tumbling down . . . Doctors told his mother he would never be more than a vegetable and advised her to admit him into a mental institution . . . Christopher is the senior class treasurer and an honor student at St. Amant High School. He believes his education is the key to achieving the life he wants to reach. He is known to inspire the entire student body. People are naturally drawn to Christopher. Christopher is known to be a speed demon, as an attempt slow him down someone taped a speeding ticket to the back of his motorized wheelchair; however, he continued to fly down the halls and remained self sufficient. He also leads a group for his other disabled classmates. Coleman wrote a book

that tells his story of living in a body that confines him. "Believe me, I understand what it feels like to have to fight. I had to fight to learn how to pick up a spoon! I had to fight to learn to sit straight in the chair! I had to fight just to learn how to open my mouth and talk. Like it or not, I had to fight to get your friendship because if I wouldn't have come up to you and said hello, you wouldn't have given me a second look. And I will have to fight the rest of my life just to be accepted in this so-called wonderful place we call America." . . . Coleman is ready to move on even though he has close bonds with the faculty at his high school.

In two weeks, I will be graduating with honors from high school. There is a feeling of excitement and nervousness in the air. I am excited because of all that I have been able to accomplish in the last four years. I'm nervous because I don't know what is next.

I know I can do this mentally, but I cannot ignore my physical limitations. I'm not sure how it is all going to work out or if it is going to work out. Do I really have what it takes to live on campus on my own? I thought about my mom. She is amazing in my book. She raised all of us by herself. We had clothes, food, and a roof over our heads at all times. I've never seen her break down. It seemed like she always had it under control. So I asked her, "How did you do it?" I was expecting to get a long list of the principles that she lived by and a step-by-step process. Instead she just told me it wasn't her; it was God. I can tell by her eyes she meant it. She wasn't just saying that to sound good. For a couple of days, her answer vexed me. I went to church with her almost every week. It seemed like at least three or four times a week she is in the kitchen cooking and singing gospel music in her own little world. But it never dawned on me this was something more than a song and dance.

In service today, they are going to mention me and the fact that I am graduating from high school. It is going to be nice to be recognized for my accomplishments. As I sit here, waiting for my name to be called, I am reflecting on all of the thoughts and events of the week. I am really scared about going off to college. I know life is going to be hard for me. Would I be able to find a job? Would I get married? How would I take care of a family? What happens to me if Momma passes away? Would my brothers and sisters take care of me? I know I can't live my whole life off disability checks. I am so nervous, and all of these questions are making me think I am going crazy. No, for real. I am not hearing voices in my head, but I am having thoughts of doing things and accomplishing things that I don't believe I can do.

CHRISTOPHER: Yes, you can do these things.

Thoughts like that. The moment I said that, the thought, "Yes, you can do these things," came into my head. I have been having an internal conflict with myself all week. I don't know what to do with this.

They are mentioning me now from the pulpit. The church is clapping for me, and the pastor is now using me as an example of what God can do in a person's life. It was a good sermon. Finally, he is wrapping it up. He is giving everybody an opportunity to come to the Lord. I don't know what is going on, but I am crying, and my wheelchair is moving forward. Where did this come from? I think I am going up to give my heart to the Lord, but I have been going to church all my life. This doesn't make sense. Besides that, I really don't like the church. All my life, they have made me feel insufficient, like I'm not good enough. Why I am doing this? But I can't stop myself. What am I doing? I can't believe I did that. I can't believe I said that. What is wrong with me? Who was that? Those questions sparked the beginning of many internal ego conflicts.

CHRISTOPHER: That was me.
CHRIS: Who are you?

CHRISTOPHER: I am you. I have been here in the background all your life. I'm the one that told Roy to stop. I am the one that raised your hand up in the air and gave you the courage to speak out loud in your algebra class. It's me that thinks it's time for you to accept Him. I am who God created you to be.

CHRIS: Why are you coming to the surface now?

CHRISTOPHER: You and society weren't ready to accept me.

CHRIS: I know society is not ready to accept you, but are you saying I am not ready to accept myself?

CHRISTOPHER: Yes, that's part of it. You have not embraced your disability yet. And because of that, you have not discovered your real gifts and abilities. You, like the rest of the world, are looking for happiness rather than pursuing joy.

CHRIS: OK, cut the crap. "Looking for happiness rather than pursuing joy," one of the same.

CHRISTOPHER: OK, you want me to cut the crap. Your life is going to be hard, and there is nothing you can do about it. That's why you need God and me to help you through this.

CHRIS: My life has always been hard. What are you talking about?

CHRISTOPHER: All week you have been torn and confused, and it's because of this reality. You haven't seen nothing yet. Whether you know it or not, Chris, you need me. You haven't been through half of the things that this world is going to put before you. You think your life has been hard, and even though a lot of things happened to you that should not have happened, you have been protected as a boy. Now you are about to go out there as a disabled black man in the South.

CHRIS: Well, I'm not sure I want you around. I think you may complicate things for me. People in this world won't like how vocal and strong you are. They expect me to be quiet and sit back in the corner.

CHRISTOPHER: Do *you* want to continue to be quiet and sit in the corner for the rest of your life?

CHRIS: Well, you said yourself, life is going to be a challenge. Why would I make it even more difficult for myself?

CHRISTOPHER: Yes, the challenges you have faced are nothing in comparison with the challenges you are going to face. Those challenges are going to come no matter what. Living your life quiet and in the corner is not going to change that. And let me be truthful with you. The way you are, you are not tough enough to deal with what is headed your way.

CHRIS: And I suppose you are going to toughen me up?

CHRISTOPHER: No, I am going to help you see that you have the necessary tools in you to become tougher than what you are now. Hopefully, I am going to help you to stop people from walking all over you.

CHRIS: Suppose that is the case, what's the other part?

CHRISTOPHER: The other part is God. Until you accept the Lord, you will never find who you really are.

CHRIS: If you are really a part of me, then you know how I feel about the church.

CHRISTOPHER: I feel the same thing too. I am probably more adamant about those issues than you will ever be. But I didn't mention the church. I said God. You need God, not the church.

CHRIS: I am not sure I am following you.

CHRISTOPHER: You, like many people, get God and the church mixed up. You blame God for the things that people have done. Our issue has not been with God and His Son. Our issue has been with His disobedient children. It's time for us to separate the two. Our freedom relies on it.

CHRIS: What's that supposed to mean?

CHRISTOPHER: A confined life is a life without belief in something greater than yourself. You will never make the transition from Chris to Christopher without meeting Christ. You must go from Chris to Christ to Christopher. People say often, "I am going to find myself." The search for self cannot be led by the individual who is lost. The individual must have someone to lead the way. Through God, you will find the courage needed to accept your disability, discover your abilities and gifts, and find out what I mean when I say pursuing joy rather than looking for happiness.

CHRIS: Momma definitely won't like you.

CHRISTOPHER: It's funny how parents teach their kids all these things and never really think about how it will play a role into developing their character. They don't realize that everything they do and teach, good or bad, will ultimately become a part of their children's adulthood. Parents tend to teach you everything you need to take on the world. They just don't think you will actually use it. But never mind all that. Even if Momma is not willing to accept me, are you willing to accept me? There are a lot of boys in this world that never truly become men because the boy in them will not accept the man in them. There are a lot of Mikes that will never become Michaels. There are a lot of Wills that will never become Williams. We have way too many Dans that will never become Daniels in this world.

Am I fooling myself? My mind is playing tricks on me right now. That's why I said I am going crazy. I just had this long conversation with myself while going through the motions of accepting the Lord. I heard someone say once that your answers come from within. However, I know even if I accept myself, society will never accept me.

CHRISTOPHER: You are always worried about what someone thinks.

CHRIS: Let's deal with one thing at a time. The truth is I have no idea what this church thing or relationship with God looks like. I do believe in Him. And I know in order for me to be where I am today, someone stronger than me had to intervene and work behind the scenes of my life through some difficult situations. But as far as what I am supposed to do, I have no idea. When the pastors come around the neighborhood, I see my aunts and uncles hide their beer cans and clean up their language. In this church, I see a lot of people just whooping and hollering and singing Hallelujah, but some of these same people I have seen drunk at my cousins' house and causing lots of fights and arguments. There are a few of them that praise God every Sunday, that have been the culprit of the very difficult situations God has brought me through. Like Mrs. Jackson over there, jumping around and shaking. They say she got the Holy Ghost. I believe it's God trying to shake the devil out of her ass. I see people looking at me out of the corner of their eye every now and then during service. I wonder if they are asking themselves, "Did he understand what I was doing on the porch that day? If so, I probably look real stupid to him right now." They would be correct in their thinking.

I didn't know that a change was supposed to happen. I thought all I had to do was say I'm sorry to God on Sunday and cover my sins up from the world, then I was OK to go on and do whatever all week. Plus I know I have to "fake it till I make it." I just have to push through this time in my life. This is the perfect answer. All I have to do is fake it until Christ comes in and helps me make it. After all, this is what everybody else is doing, right?

Your Moment with America's Unconfined Life Coach, Motivational Speaker, Author, and Confidence Builder:

Most people know in their spirit that they can do more with their lives. Some of them live their whole lives ignoring that voice inside of them. They let the reality of the moment muffle their hearts. What if by ignoring that voice no one hears and gets to know your heart?

Are you sane enough to admit that you talk to yourself?
Does your heart want to do more than your mind thinks you can do?
Can your heart truly be heard without a spiritual connection?

CHAPTER 14

Life on Campus

The Voice of Understanding: Christopher

It was time for Chris to get to know me, his other half. We had a lot to hash out over the next few years. I know the internal conflicts made him feel that he was going crazy at times, but we were actually working toward true sanity. Sometimes sanity is found in the mix of insanity. The very thing that drives you crazy can be the one thing that pushes you forward in life. It is called passion. That's the one thing that both Chris and I share.

I was having an internal ego conflict. This internal conflict happens when the mind, heart, and soul become defensive because it feels like it is being attacked. This conflict demands that the real person comes to the surface. My mind and my heart were arguing with each other. Many people would deny that they have these conversations within themselves or refuse to have them. Someone that does not have these conversations is not growing and challenging themselves toward a better life. These conversations were keys to my growth and helped me to break beyond the walls that I lived in.

Chris wasn't the only one who wasn't ready to accept me. My momma had major issues with Chris becoming Christopher. Like most mothers, she can be controlling. Also, she demands respect. Any one of my siblings would tell you, "With Momma, it's her way or the highway." If you are one of her children doing anything different from the way she would do it or doing something that she would not do, you can expect her to do and say whatever it takes to put you back in what she thinks is your place, which is under her control. It does not matter how old you are or if it hurts you, she is going to try to be in control of the situation.

Chris wants to make her proud of him. He constantly strives to hear her say "good job." And he is constantly brokenhearted because Momma is not the type of mother who validates her children's accomplishments. She always concentrates on what you should have done. Still today, Chris reminds me of what my momma would say and pulls up a picture of her face filled with anger over an understandable accident for someone with my disability. Never mind that I have found my own way of doing things. I have to do things different. My body doesn't work the same as hers and never will. Yet she will constantly demand that I do it the way that she thinks it should be done.

I know that Momma just wants me to appear as normal as possible. She wants me to move and talk like everyone else as much as possible. In her mind, she thinks constantly, telling me what I am doing wrong is training me to appear normal. I have come to realize that forcing my body to do something that it wouldn't naturally do is actually abnormal. The combination of trying to control my body with the pressure of knowing that Momma is watching my every move actually makes things more difficult for me. My older brothers, Paul and Lamont, use to tell her all the time, "He can do it. You're just making him nervous because he knows you are going to holler at him if he doesn't do it right." They were absolutely right. This is why Chris is afraid of becoming Christopher.

Momma only sees the little crippled boy in the wheelchair. She refuses to see the man that I am capable of becoming. In other words, because I have not done anything the way she would do it, she doesn't believe I can do anything, especially going off to college. Just like everyone else, she thinks I am not capable of accomplishing something this massive because of my disability. So trying to take the reins of my own life did not go over well.

I know Momma fought for me against the rest of the world. She made sure I had all life could offer me as a child with a disability. Watching her fight for me taught me how to fight for myself; now it's time that I put all that I've learned into practice. How can Momma think that after being raised under the same roof of Gladys Coleman I could just sit back and not fight for my own life? She will eventually find out that she is wrong. I will take on the world and give her a dose of her own medicine.

Let me ask you a totally ridiculous, but deep, question: Can a bird criticize a man for not being able to fly? Like I said, it is a totally ridiculous question. I know birds are not created to talk, and man is not created to fly. So would you agree with me when I say that it is ridiculous for a man to label himself or another person as disabled for not being able to do something he was not created to do? So many times we allow others to label us as being disabled or insufficient simply because we are not doing the things they feel like we should be able to do. A man that finds himself in this scenario is not weak; he is either living his life with self-inflicted failures or man-inflicted limitations. Low self-esteem, consequences of situations, and a lack of motivation are not weaknesses. There is no excuse for not being diligent and having a positive attitude. No one can say I'm not good enough or I'm not smart enough. My disability has not stopped me from setting goals and having dreams for my life.

After winning the fight with Momma to go to college, I then had to fight the fight to get into college. You would think this wouldn't be an issue because of my SAT scores and GPA; however, it was. Several colleges across the state of Louisiana did not have the facilities in their dorms to accommodate me. I traveled from one side of the state to the other side of the state trying to find a suitable campus for me. Momma was able to come on one or two of these visits, but she couldn't take many days off from work. Besides that, after she had verbally agreed to retreat and let me go to college, she still gave me some resistance. My speech therapist who has been with me all through high school was very excited about my chance to go to college; therefore, she stepped in for Momma's absence. I am so thankful for her dedication to my academic future.

I wanted to go to a major university in Baton Rouge and major in prelaw. They accepted my application without any hesitation. However, at this university I found the same problem. So, like so many other times in my life, because of my disability, I had to make a compromise. A smaller university in a nearby city agreed to house me. The truth is this university probably made a deal with the other university to prevent them from getting into any legal trouble for not having the appropriate accommodations for someone with a disability. But I am here now, and I am just going to bite the bullet and work through it. I know in my heart, if I continue to go to school here, my degree will not have the name of the university I originally wanted to attend on my degree.

It hit me in college that I am not only on the same level educationally but also chronologically. In high school, I graduated two years behind my twin sister; but in college, for many reasons, there are a lot of freshman my age or older. I no longer have to feel like I am behind and have to catch up with the rest of my peers. College is more of a challenge for me than high school. I never read anything on the college level before, but I am doing it.

I can't believe that I am actually here on campus. I can't describe what I am feeling way deep down inside. I am not nervous, I am not excited, and I am not scared. I am just in an unfamiliar environment, and I can't process it. I have never been in a place where I wasn't Gladys Coleman's disabled child or Paul and Lamont's little brother. On campus, no one knows my family. The name Coleman starts and stops here. For the first time in my life, I get to decide who Chris

Coleman is. Another thing is that everyone knows why I am here. I am not here because a program fell through or someone felt sorry for me and gave me a chance or I was promoted without doing the work to be on campus. Everyone knows that in order to be on this campus you have to have the education and the brains to be here. I don't have to prove my intelligence here. So I am kind of lost. I don't know what to do. I don't know how I am going to fit in and impress people well enough for them to like me. What am I going to do with this new environment? I've never been just Chris before. I don't know what to do to be successful or fail.

Although I feel weird and the environment is different, I love it because for the first time, I feel like I am in control of my own life. The moment I leave out of this dorm room, the decisions I make are totally up to me. I am getting my first taste of real freedom, and I like it. Boy, I've got a lot to make up for.

It turns out that I am able to fit in from one end of the spectrum to the other end. My friends Cathy, Donna, and Billy are in student government and band. They are here to get an education and be the next great something. Then there is another group I hang out with—Mark, Zack, Matt, and John, who are only here to party. Classes are their last priority. Cathy and that group love Christopher. Christopher is on campus to prove that he has the intelligence and the capability to achieve anything that he wants to do. I, Chris, fit very well in with the other group. I feel like I have to make up for lost times. I didn't have the freedom to go out and party like my other brothers and sisters did in their teenage years. I was sheltered from all of that. So it is my time to know what that life is like.

Getting my schoolwork done is a little bit challenging for me now. In high school, it was simple. I was able to copy student's notes and go back in the resource room and take tests and do homework. It doesn't work like that in college. The state provided money for me to hire someone to take me to and from classes and do homework and assignments. Now I know what it means when they say it's hard to find good help.

The first girl I hired worked out wonderfully for about two weeks. Two weeks into it, I think she picked up on the fact that I have a good heart, so eventually she started to show up late and ask me for money for gas or money to buy food for her little girl. I would give it to her and ask her to show up on time. I constantly reminded her that I needed to be in class at a certain time. I hoped that my generosity would encourage her to show the same consideration for me and my situation. However, it didn't happen that way. The next day, she came in late again. Eventually, she just didn't show up. I don't know what happened to her. Then I hired one of my buddies. Big mistake, because Luke had the same outlook on my education as he did on his own. He was here just to party, and he encouraged me to do the same. However, I know how important my education is. I like going out, but I know my education has to come first. So that didn't work out well.

Mom did not like my friends at all. She knew from the moment she came on campus for the first time that they were nothing but trouble. I can see her face, how embarrassed she was. It does not faze me at all. In my book, it is easy to embarrass my mom as her child. Just be your own person, and you'll be guaranteed to embarrass her. Besides that, I think the fact that she doesn't like them draws me even closer to that crowd.

The accommodations here are great for a person with a disability. However, for young immature adults, it is not. Because of my need for a private bathroom with a bathtub, I am living down on the bottom floor of a female dormitory. I know that a lot of guys would love to be in the predicament that I am in right now. This is going to be a fun year for me. I can tell that a lot of girls were uncomfortable with me being here at first. However, as they get to know me, I am finding out that I am an easy person to talk to. Consequently, a lot of them come to my room late at night to talk about their boyfriends or whatever was vexing them that day. Some girls in the dorm come into my room simply out of curiosity. So what do you think would happen when a young emotional curious girl gets alone with an easy-going sensitive insecure boy? It isn't long before one thing leads to another thing, and we have sex. I don't have a problem with this. Most of them are just looking for someone to talk to, and we find ourselves getting closer and more physical than we intended. It has happened enough for me to know where things are going, and I am OK with this as well. I'm fine with becoming the player that most guys want to be.

I know a lot of my friends and family are going to find this hard to believe. For some reason most of society doesn't view a person with a physical disability as a sexual being. However, that is not the case for me and many other people with disabilities. Besides that I believe that everyone whether they can be sexually active or not have a need for companionship. We all want to be held and made to feel special. A disability doesn't change that.

My promiscuous nights are now public knowledge, and I have the reputation as the big man on campus. I am not sure why I allowed this to happen or why I am getting so much pleasure out of it. It's not just the sex. There is a temporary confidence that I am getting out of these nights. Why not? It's not like I am losing my virginity. Roy had stolen that from me years ago.

As the big man on campus, guys are wanting the opportunity to hang out with me. I am becoming the most popular guy on campus. Like most of the student body, I do homework Monday through Wednesday; but Thursday through Sunday, I am out in the local bars with all the other guys, drinking, partying, and seeing who was going to get laid that night.

I am so well received in the barroom scene. Everyone seems to think it is great for someone in a wheelchair to be out on the dance floor, partying and picking up girls. I don't have to pay a dime to drink because every time I turn around, some guy is buying a drink for me. To be honest, I am loving this.

I never thought about it until this point, but I am attracted to white girls. I see a blue-eyed, milky-white-skinned brunette at the bar that I want to get to know. So far, all of my sexual experiences have been with black girls, but I am drawn to get to know this girl at the bar. At this point, I have never pursued anyone for sex or a relationship. It all just easily happens. Now I have to go up to someone and pursue. Let's see what happens.

I feel like the shy, timid, insignificant, disabled boy that the world has programmed me to feel like. My words are coming out louder, less clear, and in a stutter like they did when I was first learning how to talk. I know that anyone looking at me, thinking that I was the big man on campus, is now laughing at me. As I wait for her to walk away or respond by laughing, she gives me the biggest, most inviting smile that I ever received. As we are continuing to talk, I feel myself becoming more comfortable and loosening up. My words are becoming clearer and clearer until I think about the fact that she is talking to me or has her hand on my shoulder. This girl is actually showing me interest. It won't be just one night we did something stupid. I can tell that this is the beginning of my first relationship at twenty years of age.

Jennifer and I are having the time of our lives. The last three weeks have been amazing. She makes it known that she is with me, whether we are out partying, on campus, or in the library. She holds my hand, kisses me, and rubs my back. She lets the whole world know I am her boyfriend. This is great. The first night she came back to my dorm room, we did have sex, but it wasn't like with all the other girls. This time, it was different. This time, it was more; there was passion and excitement. We just weren't having sex just to get off. We wanted to share ourselves with each other. I fell for her hard and quick.

It felt good to be held. I never thought someone would embrace me like that ever. Even though my legs twitched and my arms constantly moved, she continued to hold me close to her; and for a moment, in between consciousness and sleep, I felt my body totally relaxed in her arms. That night was the best I have ever physically felt since the days my mom used to hold me and rock me as a child.

Now she is not returning my phone calls. She is pretending not to know me when I see her on campus or when we are out in bars or restaurants. I think the pressure of dating a black disabled man got to her. I am sure she received lots of criticisms for her choice to give me a chance that night. This really sucks. This really hurts me. This makes me want to continue my reputation as the big man on campus, and so I will continue to take advantage of these girls who just come in my room for a shoulder to cry on. However, part of me believes that they know what is going to happen at this point. I seriously doubt that the girls haven't told one another what is going on late at night in my room.

I am so surprised by my male friends. My buddies seem not to mind that I have slept with their girlfriends the night before. Not only do they not mind, some of them are encouraging me or encouraging their girlfriends to sleep with me. They think it is all a game, and that it is just so cool that I am this little slut in a wheelchair, if you will. I don't know why I was so surprised by this. The fact is, just like I didn't have much respect for these girls, their boyfriends didn't have much respect for them either. Now I have a variety of girls knocking on my door, both white and black. I think my sexual activities have gotten back to the RA and the dorm administrators because they are preparing accommodations for me in the males' dorm for next year. Meanwhile, I am going to keep enjoying the sexual liberty I have here.

The last person I hired to assist me on campus is Beth. She is working out pretty good. There is just one issue with her. I am known as a player on campus, so all of the guys are assuming that we are doing something. Beth is definitely a promiscuous girl but not on my clock. So she does not like the fact that everybody thinks that she sleeps with me. I tell all of the guys that nothing is happening, but they just don't believe me at this point.

Paul is the only one in my family that knows how my first year of college is going. I could tell him anything. And he thought it was great that I was experiencing so much. In his own words, he said, "It's time for Chris to become a man." As for Mom, I will never tell her what my college years are like. I know she doesn't like some of my friends. I don't know if she would even believe the sexual experiences that I'm having, not that I would tell her anyway. And to tell her that I am dating someone, a white girl no less, would not go over well with her, so I am just going to keep that to myself as well.

The year is ending. I have to make a decision about the summer. I don't think I can go live with my mom for three months. I have only gone home on holiday breaks and one weekend a month thus far. When I do go home, there is always an argument about who is going to take me to get my haircut or take me to church. Believe it or not, in spite of the life I am living on campus, I still feel it is important for me to go to church. You can say that I am definitely a hypocrite, but I feel a drawing to God. I am even reading the Bible every night before I go to bed, that is, if I am sober and don't have a girl in my room.

The truth is I hate going home. I feel like the family pet. My brothers and sisters have their own life, and so they don't have time to hang out with me. My mom thinks all I need is food, clean clothes, and a TV, and I should be content. I can't spend three months sitting in the house, waiting for the days to go by quickly. And besides that, she is still involved with Lee, so I am going to summer school.

My sophomore year was a lot of the same—party, drinking, party, party, and sleeping around with different girls. It is ironic how much I am partying and still able to keep my grades up.

Sleeping around isn't quite as easy as it was last year because they moved me out of the girls' dormitory. However, girls still find their way into my room—whether it is through the front door for everyone to know or through my window so their boyfriends wouldn't find out. Classes are a little difficult. I am definitely not making all A's, but I am doing pretty well. Everything is now a routine for me. This is going to be my life for the next four years, so I thought.

I did something the other day that I hate myself for. It proves that I am the piece of garbage that the world has always told me I was. What I did, I will never forgive myself for. I can't believe I did this. I don't know how I am going to deal with what is going on inside of my head now. In the male dormitory, there are community showers, which are working fine for me because they put a bench in the showers. I have to be careful not to slip and fall, but for the most part, I can handle getting in and out of the shower without hurting myself. When I went in a couple of days ago, before pulling myself up into the shower, I looked at a guy on the opposite end of the showers. It wasn't just a quick glance. I actually took a few seconds out of my day and looked at him.

That one look has sparked many different sexual thoughts as well as emotional feelings over the last few days. The reality of this freaked me out. Where did that come from? What am I thinking? Why am I feeling this way? Why did I look? I don't know what I am going to do with this. I can't have issues like this. I am going too far. I have to straighten my life up somehow.

I can't even tell Paul about this. He would be so disappointed in me. He probably won't even talk to me again. I don't understand why I am thinking like this. I know what is right. A man is not supposed to have these thoughts and desires. I will not let this happen to me. I spent too many days being looked down upon because of my disability. I cannot deal with the possibility of people finding out I could be gay or bisexual. I have to change something, and I have to change it right now. Please, God, show me a way out of this. I know this is not what you want for me either.

CHRISTOPHER:	What are you doing?
CHRIS:	I'm living my life.
CHRISTOPHER:	Well, you are destroying my life.
CHRIS:	Dealing with the things I had to face is destroying my life.
CHRISTOPHER:	You can't blame yourself for things you could not control.
CHRIS:	I know that. But the questions are still there: How would my life be different if I had a father? What if my mom was able to stay at home and raise me like

many mothers? Why did it take so long for people to realize that I was understanding everything that was going on around me? Why did my body react to something I obviously hated in my mind? Am I gay or bisexual? Why did God put me into this body and allow me to go through these difficult challenges in my life? Am I right or wrong for questioning my life and having these thoughts and feelings?

CHRISTOPHER: The questions you are having now are because you are trying to live your life as if the last twenty years did not happen.

CHRIS: Wrong. I'm questioning this, because the last twenty years did happen.

———◆———

Your Moment with America's Unconfined Life Coach, Motivational Speaker, Author, and Confidence Builder:

In some situations, what is right for one person can be wrong for another. People who have a hard time accepting themselves have embraced the standards and convictions of another. But the highest standard a person could have is to become his own person and to live out their own convictions.

When do you find yourself going back to being who everyone expects you to be?

What type of environment do you need to be in to be you?

What are you doing today, only because of yesterday?

CHAPTER 15

Grow Up and Live Out

The Voice of Understanding: Christopher

History is history for a reason. Most people study it to learn from it, but that is not typically what we do with personal history, is it? We use our personal history as a vision for our future. We don't learn from it; we decide to live by it, to remain in an emotional rut. Why do we do this? Because we don't want to take the time to unpack the pain and the hurt of the past. We would rather hold onto the ball and chain, but the ball and chain is not holding us back; we are pulling them forward. We are the ones who chose not to detach our self from them. The ball and chain become our identity. Moving on means to take an action that forces us to arise from our emotional rut and seek progress in our lives. It's about separating ourselves from the issues that hold us back.

A confined life is a life prevented from making mistakes. There needs to come a time in every young person's life where their family and friends cannot protect them from learning the hard lessons of becoming a man or woman. We all need the freedom to make mistakes in order to develop the ability to grow. Growth is the result of lessons from our mistakes. A disability did not excuse me from this fact. I had to spend some time with the wrong friends, the crazy crowds, and the wild girls.

I will be the first to admit I am not proud of Chris' decisions at this time of our life. The relationship Chris established with all these girls had nothing to do with them. The truth is Chris was trying to prove something to himself. Having gone through sexual abuse was still a big issue for us. These sexual encounters with women from the dorm were his way, in his mind, to prove he wasn't gay or bisexual. He used these girls for psychological healing. He did not realize that was only going to happen through years and years of dealing with the issue that he continued to avoid. A part of me also wanted to prove to these curious girls that I was just the same as the next guy.

That only scratched the surface of what is really going on in us. We have to deal with the pain of our past and the struggles associated with having a disability. The longer we hold it in, the more it's eating us alive. It's only making things worse. To tell you the truth, we are more worried about the response of other people than healing from the abuse.

Someone that knows Christ as their Lord and Savior doesn't need to speak of these things, right? Somewhere along the way, it's been said, "Just give it over to God and move on." That's what I've been taught. Just pray about it. Keep it quiet. It will all work itself out. Now I am starting to realize that is literally true. The things we try to hold on to and bottle up inside for years will eventually work itself out. Things are starting to unravel and the hurt, pain, disappointment, and shame is beginning to rise to the surface.

There are situations in our lives that we hang on to as if we are locked to them. We choose to hang on to these situations because of fear rather than reaching out for true healing. Even though we see that the rope we are hanging on to is slowly ripping, we pretend that we are chained to it and take the chance of falling. We would rather hang there and try to pry our way out rather than acknowledging it is just a weak rope and cut ourselves loose. All I had to do was get the help I needed to be free from this bondage. But out of fear of how society would respond, I kept myself chained to the past.

Chris thought he was going crazy two years ago when he heard a voice inside of his head, but now he is convinced he is going crazy because now he hears two different voices in his head. On top of this, one of them has made a life-changing decision for him. Let me explain. It all started about three months ago. He took this class called technical writing. What we did was learn the legalities of writing a technical manual. There is actually a standard you must follow when writing a manual to prevent the user of the machinery from suing the company because of something they weren't aware of. I loved this class, so I decided that I was going to do some research and see how I could learn more about this field.

A couple of weeks later, I was out in the local bar with some of my friends, getting ready to take my first drink for the night. Then I heard a voice in my head. It wasn't Christopher or Chris; it was a different voice, a male voice. And He said, "Yep, this is why I saved you. So you can throw my blood back into my face." I can take all of the creative writing classes in the world and still not be able to describe to you the feeling I got in the pit of my stomach. Right then and there, I looked at my friends and said, "I got to go. I don't care if y'all stay. I don't care if y'all party all night, but I don't belong here. I have to go." The drinking, the partying, and the girls came to a screeching halt.

About three days after that, I received a letter in the mail from an university in Georgia. I honestly have no idea how they got my information. I have never heard of this school before that letter came to my mailbox. But low and behold, it was a letter telling me about their technical and professional communication major, along with a catalog. I had no intention of moving out of Louisiana. I know I needed to be close to my family for them to help me take care of myself, but at the same time, I was looking for something. I knew that my life on campus now had to drastically change.

I planned a trip to Atlanta, Georgia, one weekend. Don't ask me what I was thinking. I had no connections in Georgia. I didn't even know how I was going to get to the campus, but I decided to get on a plane and fly to Atlanta, into the biggest airport I have ever been in. Somehow I found my way through the airport, caught a taxicab, and paid $45 for them to take me to the campus. Then I met with the dean of disability, looked around the campus, and flew back that Sunday. When I got back, I started right away getting ready for my classes the next week. It was a fun adventure, but nothing more than that. I just went on with my schooling.

A man who hasn't been challenged to grow up and live out what he believes is living a confined life. About two weeks ago, that voice came back into my head and said, "Move to Marietta, Georgia." Some people think I am joking, but I literally looked up toward heaven and motioned to God with my index finger to come here. At that moment, a three-way conversation began.

CHRISTOPHER: We have to have a talk, God.

CHRIS: I can't do this. Just look at me.

GOD: I don't have to look at you. I made you.

CHRIS: This is not going to be easy. Momma is going to flip out. Do you think she's really going to just let me up and move to Marietta, Georgia?

CHRISTOPHER: She has to get over it.

GOD: Go. This is what I have called you to do. Don't worry about what anyone is going to say.

I don't know why we decided to do this. Maybe Chris is trying to run away from his pain and all the mistakes he made. Or is it because I know that I can accomplish so much more with my life, and this may be the next step to do it? Or just maybe Chris and I agreed to take a leap of faith and believe that God is calling us to move to Marietta, Georgia? Whatever the reason is, I am moving this year.

Everyone thought I was out of my mind moving to Georgia. They felt like I didn't know what I was getting into. They thought I was setting myself up to be physically in danger and to experience some personal heartbreaks. All that was true except one part. I was not out of my mind. Before moving, I thought about everything they were saying intently. After evaluating my past, looking at where I was, and trying to predict the future, I came to the following conclusions.

When I graduate I still would not have the support I will need to get back and forth in order to pursue a professional and personal life. As soon as I move off campus back to my mom's house, my life would be over. Momma, over the years, has communicated her inability to stand by my side as I grow from a boy into manhood. She feels that she is too old to physically transport me from one place to the next. Not only that, she also thinks that I expect too much out of life for a person with a disability. She believes that I should settle for a safe and clean environment. Anything beyond that, I should not want. My older brother Lamont and his wife would take me in and allow me to live in their home, but that would only come after Momma's death. For now, they feel its Momma's responsibility to take care of me.

Over the last ten years Paul has been living a hard and harder life due to his deep involvement in this rough community. Dewayne and Russell are not that far behind him. Dewayne wouldn't ever slow down to take care of me, and Russell is a professional con artist. My two sisters, Angela and Christina, are trying to find their own way in life. I know that they do not have the personal clarity in their lives needed to support me and my life.

I was so sick of Mom being on top of my every move. I understand, especially as a disabled child, there is a time of training, a time of making sure that child is growing properly and learning the proper etiquette and the proper way of doing things. But my physical progress came to a halt. I am not going to talk any clearer. I am not going to move quite like the next person. I am not going to be able to hold my feet perfectly straight at all times. There came a point in my life when I was more confined by trying to look normal than I was by just being who God created me to be.

Your Moment with America's Unconfined Life Coach, Motivational Speaker, Author, and Confidence Builder:

I believe we are all born with faith. The challenge is what we will do with that faith. A wise person never put it all in one basket. If we have spiritual faith, personal faith, and faith in mankind, then one will prevail when the others fail you.

What are you doing with your history?
Is it not time for a change?
Are you afraid to take a leap of faith?

CHAPTER 16

The Big Move

The Voice of Experience: Chris

Mid-August of 1995, my brothers Dewayne, Paul, and Lamont and my twin sister Christina packed up the car, rented a van, and drove me out to Georgia. Mom said she just couldn't stand leaving me there, so she did not come. It was probably one of the best times I could ever remember us having as a family. In the eight-hour drive, we laughed and talked and joked around. Paul and Lamont teased each other all the way there. When we got to Atlanta, the first place we went was the underground. We did a lot of shopping and just hung out as a family. That trip was the closest thing to a family vacation we ever had.

Once we got on campus, Christina initiated a cleanup. She was not going to leave my dormitory in the condition it was in. So everybody chipped in and got to work cleaning. All of a sudden, I heard a window sliding down quickly and my brother Dewayne saying, "Blank, blank." The window slammed down on his middle finger. The dull, corroded, metal frame managed to cut halfway into his finger. Unfortunately, this is no surprise. Dewayne tends to always get himself hurt, from a burn he got very early on as a child all the way to slicing his foot halfway off with a chainsaw. This is my brother Dewayne, always finding a way to hurt himself. After we got him situated, we proceeded to clean up my dormitory, and within hours, everything was done. Then my brothers and sister got back in their car and left.

The move away from my family introduced me into a whole new world with new choices and new possibilities. I had to decide on my future. Venturing out on my own forced me to know God. Not just believe in Him, I had to know what I believed about Him and why I believed it. Sitting there all by myself, I started to think about what was actually happening.

CHRIS: I want to go home.
GOD: I got a plan for your life.
CHRIS: That's fine, God, but can You work out that plan in Baton Rouge, Louisiana? I want to go home.
GOD: I have a plan for your life.

This move is not just about getting away from my family and the mistakes I have made over the last two years of college. It is about truly starting over. It is about getting away from all of the disappointment that surrounds me in Louisiana. There I am constantly reminded that my father chose not to be a part of my life. Roy is still hanging around as if nothing ever happened. Thank God my mom finally chose to break up with him and marry someone else after all these years, but the memories of him linger in that house. I want to be free from all of that. It's like I am constantly living under a wet blanket there. Here in Georgia, I truly have a chance to start a new life. But I can't help but ask myself, *What in the hell am I doing here?*

Still I knew I had to detach myself from my family. I could no longer be emotionally tied to them. I had to find a place where I could thrive and reach my true potential. I had to establish my own roots. Establishing my own roots is the step that I failed to follow through with for a long time. I figured because I was in Georgia, there was no need for me to go any farther. My unsettled emotions continued to dictate my life. What I have learned over time is complacency allows the past to catch up with us.

Maybe I just need to get out of this dorm room and stop thinking about the fact that I am now in Georgia and my family is on their way back to Louisiana, soon to be seven hundred miles away from me. As I open my door and just sit there, I watch the other students bring loads and loads of stuff into their rooms. I smile and wave to a couple of them, and they wave back. Oh well, I am here now. Let's see what happens.

This university is the perfect place for me to start this new life. It is a very hard school and has few girls because it has a technological focus. They are trying to keep up with other engineering schools in the state. Therefore, it is a very serious campus to live on. Not much playing and partying goes on here. It's all about getting your education. The drinking, the partying, and the sex with girls are now over. As far as I am concerned, God is telling me, "Enough is enough. This is not my plan for your life. I am calling you to do something great. So stop it!" And that is all right by me. I know now that life wasn't for me anyway.

One thing that has not changed, and unfortunately will probably never change, is the ignorant view people have on a person with a disability. I still have to deal with those people that will always come up to me and talk in a loud voice as if I can't hear them. Sometimes I just want to say to them, "Hold up. Let me turn up my wheelchair so I can hear you better." And then there are those who think the only way they can communicate with me is to talk to me as if I am on a kindergarten level. My all-time favorite is the waiter who sees me communicating with the people at my table and still finds it necessary to ask one of them what I want to drink.

Just the other day, I went to the market for food and other things I needed in my dorm. I jumped on the public bus. From the bus stop, I had to go about a half a block up to the market. Once I got there, I proceeded to gather up the things I needed into my lap, take it to the checkout line, and waited to be checked out. The lady behind the counter just stood there waiting. Finally, she asked me, "Is your mom and dad coming soon?"

To which I told her, "I am not with my mom or dad."

She then asked, "Oh, what about your legal guardian or caretaker? Are you in a group home?"

To which I responded, "No. I am here on my own. Can I pay for my purchases?"

She refused to believe that I was telling her the truth and continued to wait for someone to take up the financial responsibility for my purchases. Finally, the manager came over; and I was able to communicate to him that I was in college, I took a bus here, and these are the things I decided I wanted to purchase. And believe it or not, I had the money to do so. I am tired of being treated like an idiot by idiots.

Another observation I have made over the past few months is that some people will always mentally check out on me long before taking the time to understand my cognitive abilities. They will look at my wheelchair and automatically assume that they cannot communicate with me because of my physical limitations. They do not understand that cognitive abilities are not connected to the physical abilities. Yet they think I am the one that needs help. By the time I get the first word out of my mouth, they have already decided that they cannot understand me. I know that this is a decision they have mentally made based on their lack of understanding of the disabled population. As a matter of fact, there are many people who meet me for the first time in a loud environment who are still able to hear and understand me clearly. For the most part, it's the mentality of the society that decides if my disability is going to cause a communication breakdown or not.

Don't bother with trying to understand me, because I'm different from you. My words will never be clear to you. The essence of who I am could never contribute to who you are. So just shove me into a corner. Pretend like I don't exist, because I am different from you.

Don't bother with trying to understand me. I will never fit in your box. I will never live up to your standards and live out your convictions. You have every right to judge me. Who cares if your lack of understanding creates barriers for me? That's what I get for being different from you.

Just know that I understand you. I understand you, my friends and family. I understand you, my religious and spiritual leaders. I understand you, my teachers and wise counselors. I understand you, my government officials and rule makers. You are a part of a society that trains bullies by example and then punishes them for putting that training to practice. You and society are the bullies we are desperately trying to keep children away from. The two of you have skillfully taught generation after generation how to alienate people and devalue the lives of others. You and society together are the masters of all bullies. A bully only bullies someone they don't understand because that someone is different from them.

Until you can ignore our minute differences and embrace our many similarities, don't try to understand me, but do understand that you have taught me the importance of being different from you. Understanding people's differences has given me a different understanding. The answers and the truths you are looking for, I have found buried beneath the things you refuse to understand. What you see as different and useless, I understand to be rare and therefore priceless. Thank God I am different from you.

We cannot tolerate the things that we simply do not understand. And that's OK as long as we understand that we also cannot judge the things that we have not taken the time out to understand. It takes an arrogant and self-righteous person to judge something they do not understand. Yes, God gave us permission to discern and know people by the fruit of their spirits, but when we refuse to take time out to understand the roots of their fruit, then we have no right to judge them.

My brother Lamont and his wife came to visit recently. I am not surprised he was the first. I knew that it wouldn't be long before he had to check in and see for himself how I was doing. Lamont was always worried about my physical well-being. Paul would have come too, but drugs are getting the best of him right now. Momma probably said she was coming this time and backed out at the last minute. She hates to travel. We talk every week, but I know she wonders how I am really doing. Hopefully, Lamont felt like he could give her a good report. He seemed pleased with me.

People are starting to ask where I come from and what I am doing here. One lady said, "Your mom must be very proud of you." I was prepared for a lot of things, but I wasn't prepared for that. The truth was if my mom is proud of me in any way, shape, or form, she has not communicated that yet. As far as I know, she is waiting for me to call home and say, "I failed. Come and get me." But that will never happen. No matter what I face, no matter what happens, I will not go home.

I felt like I had to come up with a response to this statement, "Your mom and family must be very proud of you." I was too embarrassed to say, "I really don't know." I know my brothers want me to gain as much independence as possible. Paul, Lamont, Dewayne, and even Russell are happy that I took this step; but as far as being proud of me, I can only speak for Paul and Lamont. So my fake-it-till-I-make-it mentality kicked in, and I said, "Yes."

My momma would say, "That is not the way I raised you." My fake-it-till-I-make-it mind-set is not something I should be embracing. Parents need to learn one very valuable lesson about parenting. Their son or daughter may not always do what they tell them to do nor will he/she always mimic what they show them. However, the experience they go through and the things that parents expose them to will forever affect their kids. The experiences that parents subject their children to are also tools for raising that child.

I did exactly what my momma did to get where she is in life. I proceeded to paint the perfect picture of a perfect family in which I came from. I made my family into the family I thought they should have been all along: more loving and supporting. Though they had those characteristics in them, it definitely wasn't the cornerstone of my family. I am not ashamed of them, but I do wish we were the close-knit family we once were. I am also hurt by their lack of involvement in my life. That is one of the reasons I am here trying to build a life without them.

Almost instantly, Michael, Steven, Ricky, and Andrew became my new best friends. They are all younger Christians. This put my mind at ease. I know I can fit into this crowd. I know exactly what they expect. I believe in God as well, so it won't be hard to continue faking it until I make it. I took what was already an amazing story and dramatized it. I told my new Christian friends the story I wanted them to hear and the things I thought they needed to know in order to accept me into their clique. And it worked. I am heavily involved in the BSU (Baptist Student Union) on campus. We're all different, but everyone likes me here. This is so different from the first two years of college. This is why I decided to stick to my story.

I thought I had a strong relationship with Christ, but after moving to Georgia and living on my own, that is now being put to the test. First, I allowed someone to take advantage of my heart. My assistant,

Jacob, needed money to do some car repair, so he said. I didn't realize that he was fully aware that this was the beginning of a new semester, and I would have extra money to live off from the remainder of my student loan. Nevertheless, I let him borrow $1,500. And part of me really believed he was really going to pay me back, but after asking him about it for the last two weeks, he has totally disappeared and I can't find him anywhere.

A few weeks ago, I felt myself coming out of a deep sleep. The closer I got to the surface of being awake, the more I felt awkward and in pain. My face felt heavy and blown up. Every time I took a deep breath, I felt a sharp pain in my side. Eventually, I heard a constant beeping and the sound of a pump. As I opened my eyes, I could see through a glass door in which there were many people walking back and forth from one room to the next room to the middle counter and back around again. I was in the emergency room. I thought to myself, *What is going on?*

I remembered the night before, hearing someone climbing into my dorm window. I tried to pull myself out of my deep sleep and figure out what was going on, but before I could do it, he had me pinned down. "Are you OK?" a nurse asked me as she walked into my room. "Do you have any idea who did this to you?"

"No," I responded as she poured pills into my mouth and held up a cup of water with a straw to my lips.

"Well, you are going to be just fine," she said as she walked back out of the room. *I am not going to be fine*, I thought to myself.

CHRISTOPHER: Yes, you are. This is just a little setback.
CHRIS: This is not just a little setback. Things like this keep happening time and time again, and I am getting tired of it. I want to go home.
CHRISTOPHER: You cannot call Momma or anyone. You know they will be up here in a heartbeat and haul you back to Louisiana.

CHRIS:	I know. That's what I want. I am ready to go. I am tired of this. I just want to go back home.
CHRISTOPHER:	And do what, sit in the house for the rest of your life?
CHRIS:	Well, it is a lot better than this.
CHRISTOPHER:	Really, is that what you want? Do you really want to sit, watch TV, and rot for the rest of your life? Is that why you worked so hard to get to where you are now? To let something this stupid stop you from moving forward? You know God is going to do something big in your life. That is why you came to Georgia.
CHRIS:	I know I can't call anyone. You're right. But I am so mad and so disappointed. I am tired of fighting against everyone, just so I can live. Why did this have to happen? God, do you know how hard this is?
CHRISTOPHER:	This is one of those times I understand why you want to give-up. But, you can't.

My friend Andrew from the dormitory walked in and asked, "Can I do anything for you? Can I call your mom?"

"No. Don't call her. I'm fine."

"You sure?" he asked.

Just like I told so many friends of mine after I have a seizure, I said, "Don't call her. All she would want to do is pick me up and move me back to Louisiana. That is no life for me. Just get me home and don't tell anyone else about this."

A few hours later, I was released from the emergency room. There was a small investigation on campus, but they didn't find out anything, and I didn't pursue it because I didn't want anyone to know and make a bigger deal out of it. Though it bothered me, over the years I became very good at giving myself prep talks. I knew I just had to keep on going and push through. Three days later, I was back in class, pressing forward like I've always done.

Your Moment with America's Unconfined Life Coach, Motivational Speaker, Author, and Confidence Builder:

There comes a time in life where a person has to allow perseverance and determination to take over. Your emotions and feelings have to take a back seat in order for you to move forward in life.

What if the change you are waiting for never happens?
Are you looking for acceptance from people who can't understand you?
What in your past are you allowing to catch up with you?

CHAPTER 17

How Much More?

The Voice of Experience: Chris

After being in Georgia for a few months, I thought it was important that I start counseling. I wanted to talk out these thoughts that I had inside of my head. I told the Christian counselor everything. From the moment I was born, everything I could remember, everything that bothered me, everything that went wrong, everything that people said and did around me. I told him about the things Roy did to me.

Now I realize that Roy was only doing these things because I was weak. He thought my disability gave him permission to do those things. If I was anyone else or able to talk or move around more, if I was emotionally able to deal with the consequences of telling someone what he was doing, he would have never abused me all those years. But it is too late now. I also know I had to keep it a secret for the sake of Momma and my brothers. Paul, Lamont, Dewayne, and Russell may have their own lives; but they love me. They wanted to protect me as their little brother. I know one of them would have ended up in prison. I had to hold this secret within me. Holding this secret in me all these years made me feel like Roy never stopped. Many days I felt like Roy was still using the bathroom on me.

When I told my counselor of all of the sexual feelings and thoughts that were going on inside of my head, he said because of all the things that happened, that it was OK for me to have these thoughts in my head. My response to that was, "No, it is not OK. I am a man and a Christian. I should not have these thoughts in my head." Besides that, I am a black disabled Christian in the South; I can't have these thoughts in my head. My friends, family, and church will never ever excuse me from these thoughts, no matter what happened in the past. God can forgive the man that killed another person. God can forgive a man that has an affair on his wife. But as far as homosexuality or bisexuality, God's grace stops there. That is an unforgivable sin according to the church. I know it. The church has taught me that this is an abomination. This is perverse, and God will not accept that. God will not forgive a man for this.

So I stopped going to the sessions. I decided I could not continue talking with him. I am going to dive into the Bible. I am going to clean up my thought life, and I am going to be very careful not to allow this to creep back into my life. I won't live with the bisexual or gay label on top of a disability. I am bound and determined that this will not be the case in my life. Meanwhile, until I heal, this is just another shameful thing in my life that I have to keep covered up. I will fake it till I make it.

I didn't know I would come to a point that my fake-it-till-I-make-it mind-set would be shattered. But here I am. I never thought I would be at this place in my life, but I am and there is nothing I can do about it. No one understands that. I have let them down and disappointed them so much that they no longer care about me. The only thing they acknowledge is the fact that I am here and what that means to them. They are not concerned about what drove me here, or whether or not they could have prevented me from getting here. They have ignored the fact that so many things have occurred in my life, especially over the last few years, that it literally pushed me to this place.

To begin with, I suddenly woke up with the pain of having my father reject me. The truth is I never said it, but it is eating me up that he chose not to be a part of my life. When I think about it, I can't help but ask myself, "What did I ever do to him?" It seemed like he pursued a relationship with my twin sister and all of his other kids, but not me. On top of that, I wonder how different my life would have been if he stayed around. Maybe I wouldn't have been abused. Maybe they would have found out early on that there was more going on in my mind than people were giving me credit for. Maybe my family would not have been quite as overwhelmed with having to take care of me. Maybe Momma would have had the financial help that she needed, and Paul would have never gotten so deeply involved in that toxic community. I am so damn angry at my father!

Speaking of Paul, he is not doing too well. That community has eaten him alive. He used to be this big strong solid guy, and now he looks like a pencil. We don't talk too much because he disappears for weeks and weeks at a time. When he does come back, he doesn't want us crowding him and asking him where he was. I so wish I could help him, but I can't. I have to watch him continue to destroy his life. Momma tried to pretend that Paul's problems aren't getting the best of her. But the truth is we all are so very worried about what's going to happen to him. The sad part is Dewayne and Russell don't realize that Paul has ruined his life, and if they keep down the same track, they will do the same thing. I am wondering what has to happen for them to change.

I wonder, does my mom realize it was just as hard for us to watch her get involved with Lee as it is for her to watch some of her kids get involved this community? The end result is the same. Both parties are watching someone they love and care about get torn down and run the risk of possibly losing their life. I still have nightmares. I remember vividly the chaos that my mom's ex-boyfriend, Lee, caused. So many times I worried about how far things would go before someone got seriously hurt or worse. I thought because I was out of Louisiana, those memories would fade away.

I still wake up afraid as if I am right there in the moment. So many things are going through my mind. I cannot understand what Mrs. Smith was thinking and why Roy had to do those things to me. The combination of counseling and becoming an adult makes me understand now that they had to somewhat know of the long-term effect that it would have on my life. I just don't understand what they were thinking. There are days now I think about ways I could have killed them both and gotten off for it. At that age, I just wasn't thinking along those lines. Thank God for that.

I was trying to finish my last year of college when all of these thoughts and emotions came to the surface. I was carrying a full load of classes, and it seemed like the hardest semester I have ever had. It was hard not because of the workload, but because it was the start of a whole new chapter of my life, that the world wasn't ready for me to start. I know even though I have a good education and would be a good employee, the possibility of me finding a job in technical writing is very small, not because there is not enough work out there, but because the individual who would be interviewing me would probably not see past my disability. I know I am going to have to fight to get them to see that I am more than capable of doing the job. This is not a small issue. If I can't support myself, I will have to move back home, and that is the last thing I want to have to think about.

On the upstream, I am very involved in a large Baptist church in the South. The people here treat me very well. They have even bought me a new manual wheelchair because mine was falling apart, but I knew in my heart, if they knew all the things I have been through and am going through, they would not look at me the same way. As long as I appear to be this perfect Christian boy in the wheelchair, everything will be great. But what would happen if they knew my background and how I crawled my way out of a dark hole?

What would happen if they knew I had sexual thoughts and wasn't sure of my sexuality?

I know there will be many people who don't understand what I had to go through to be where I am today. Those same people will turn around and judge the things I have done wrong. They will not inquire about the number of things I had to do right to be here in spite of my mistakes. I know in my heart that they won't look at me the same way.

I decided about halfway through my senior year that I wanted to move out of the dormitory, especially after what happened to me there. So Mike, a friend from the singles group, and I got an apartment not too far from campus. I knew something wasn't quite right with him. I understood that Mike was on medication for bipolar, but he seemed to be a pretty stable guy who was welcomed in the singles group. I felt like he genuinely cared about me, and so he would make a great roommate. One day, I started to feel bad from all the pressures of life. I knew I was going into a seizure, so I lay down for the night, expecting to wake up in the middle of the night on the floor, as I have done so many times before.

When I did wake up, I was actually in my bed, but I knew something was different with this seizure. I didn't feel the same. I wanted to cry so bad, and I didn't know why. You know how some things just jog your memory? You watch a movie or listen to a sound or read a certain line in a book, and all of a sudden, a memory comes back. It's almost like our subconscious locks it away to where we can't pull it up anymore, and all of a sudden, out of the blue, we find the key to that lock. That day, I had the lock on my memory opened.

I remembered the first time I cried over the things Roy did to me. My aunt was babysitting me while Momma was at work. I wasn't feeling well enough to be in school. While sitting there watching TV, I heard my aunt let out a loud scream. I heard a loud thump, and it seemed like someone was trying to tear down the walls in her bedroom. I heard the breaking of glass hitting the floor. I got off the couch, crawled around the corner, where her bedroom door was slightly open. There I saw her lying halfway off the bed. I thought she was dead with her eyes open, but the tears running down her face indicated that she was still alive, but her body just laid there lifeless as this man thrust himself against her over and over.

I remember crawling off into another room and telling myself it was OK to cry. Her lying there lifeless was a live symbol of what I've been feeling every time Roy came around. I cried, cried for my aunt, cried for my pain, cried for her pain. For the first time in my life, I felt like I knew someone who knew what I was going through, someone who knew what it felt like to be alive but lifeless, to be filled with working organs yet dead inside.

The morning after that seizure, I felt a physical pain that I had not felt after a seizure. It was a familiar pain, but not the type of pain I had from a seizure. This pain was in my lower rectum. I can't prove it, but Mike did something to me that night. I know it. I felt it in my heart. It was all too much a familiar atmosphere to me. I knew I have been there before. I didn't know how to deal with this. I felt like I was going to break. This affected me differently. I am not only mad about it, but I am embarrassed of it as well. I feel like I should have done something to protect myself. I wanted to believe, because I was in a different state and in a different environment, this could never happen again. I mean I'm not just in a different environment. I am surrounded by Christians who I thought would never do something like this. I was wrong. I wish I could have protected myself or have done something to stop it from happening. In 1994, Roeher Institute in Ontario, Canada, reported that men with disabilities are twice as likely to be sexually abused in their lifetime as men without disabilities.

I called my singles pastor and told him what I believed happened. He sent a friend of mine to pick me up, and Mike disappeared. I never saw him again, not even in a church service. Deep down inside, I was hoping that I would see him. I was hoping that he would argue with me or tell me that it didn't happen. The fact that he was no longer around makes me think that something similar must have happened before or he didn't dispute it when they confronted him on it.

I don't know who in the singles group knew about what Mike did, but here is what I do know. The church and everyone there expected me to smile and shout hallelujah and just say, "God is sufficient," and not communicate any of my pain, hurt, or aggravation. I am a Christian hero in their eyes. And what makes me a hero is the fact that I am living up to their expectations. The truth is they enjoy seeing me smiling in my suffering because it makes them feel better about their lives. I can't dare show any weakness or vulnerability.

I feel like I am in a cage in the middle of a great big amusement park. The park is full of people freely enjoying all of the activities and rides that were available to them. Every now and then, they come over and look at me, an animal that is on display for the world to see. They will feed me, pet me, and even talk to me. But they wouldn't dare let me out of the cage.

I should have never opened myself up. I let people get too close to me. This is why he took advantage of my situation. I hate to have to express my feelings this way, but I am so damn mad. This is bullshit! This has damaged and weighed on my heart now more than anything that has happened in the past. I am mad at him, and I am mad at myself. I am not a nine-year-old boy anymore. I am a twenty-four-year-old man, and this has happened. I am pissed off and really confused. Is there something about me that gives off the impression that it is OK or that I would somehow like this? Why did this happen again? Why did I trust him in the first place? I spent months and months asking myself that.

This incident re-sparked the mental struggle with my sexual identity. It escalated and manifested itself through the Internet. I found myself on various sites from heterosexual to bisexual to homosexual material. I knew mentally I was going down the wrong path, and I wanted desperately to stop. So I went back to counseling.

I stayed in it for a long time, until they told me that I had to tell my momma what happened. I didn't think it was necessary to bring that much pain into her life. In Georgia, it is just me. I am the only one that has to be affected by this. My life in Louisiana is what I am trying to let go of. And, frankly, I just don't want to deal with it. I don't want to deal with any of this unnecessary shit. It is not right, and it is not fair, and I am tired of it.

Your Moment with America's Unconfined Life Coach, Motivational Speaker, Author, and Confidence Builder:

It doesn't matter what your spiritual beliefs are; life still happens. We also cannot fake our way through hardship and just wait for a change to happen. What we can do is put it all out there and deal with it. Our desire to change things and our spiritual beliefs has to become our motivation to face adversity head-on.

Are you still living with the pain of your childhood?
What are you tired of dealing with?
Are you hurting yourself by protecting someone else? If so, why?

CHAPTER 18

Taking Life Back

The Voice of Experience: Chris

From the very beginning, I was told that I was "special" because of my physical insufficiency according to society. This mind-set resulted in me trying to hide my weakness and show people only what I thought they would accept. Right away, we built a relationship on false pretenses. I only showed people one-third of me because I felt they would not accept the other two-thirds.

I remember as a boy asking myself and thinking: *"Who am I? What am I?"* When they look in my eyes, they say, "Chris, Baby, Buddy, Little Man." Whatever they call me, I know I'm not one of them. I don't move like they do. I can't talk like they do. They relate to me differently than they relate to one another. I think they like me. They are smiling at me and talking softly, sweet, and funny. I want them to know I can hear them. I want to smile and talk to them, but I can't. Do they know I understand them? How do I reply? I feel removed from their world. They are free. I am trapped, trapped in a body that will not allow me to move or communicate."

I know who I am now. I am the unlovable. Look at whom the world defines as sufficient. Think about what we consider as strength and weakness in America. Look at the way the world labels and treats someone with a disability. I have come to grips with the way people have treated me in the past and have realized that I am the unlovable.

I tried so hard not to ask this question, but now I have to ask, Why me? Why do I have to be the one that is going through all of this? I am not looking for sympathy. I am looking for answers. I have to be truthful. I don't understand why I am at this place in my life.

All of this is weighing on me like a ton of bricks. It's so hard to deal with all of things that are happening. I am just so tired of this. I'm tired of fighting. It seems like every time I try to move forward in my life, someone pushes me in the corner and makes me feel like I'm not deserving of living a full life. Every time I tried to become Christopher, someone diminishes me to Chris. I can never be that nine-year-old insecure boy again. But because of my disability, society will not allow me to be the twenty-five-year-old man I'm becoming. Here I am months before graduating from college, I have beaten all the odds, and I still have to worry about someone taking away my freedom and making me feel insufficient. I couldn't take that anymore. I'm tired of fighting and crawling my way out of a cage. Out of the cage everyone else wants me to live in. I'm no longer trapped by my circumstances. I'm trapped by people's perspective of a person with a disability.

So tonight, I just gave up. I called a friend to say bye, locked my bedroom door, swallowed some pills, and turned off all the lights. I wanted to put an end to it all. So here I am now, on the bed of the emergency room, as the nurse and doctor pump my stomach from all of the medication I purposely took. I'm thinking, *Where do I go from here? They can pump out my stomach, but they can't pump out the crap poured into my life. Do I even want to get back up and fight again? Life will surely knock me back down just like it has every time I try to get up. Yes, I give up. This time, I am done. Why go on?*

CHRISTOPHER:	What do mean, "why go on?" Why did you do that?
CHRIS:	Because I'm tired. People don't understand that life is hard. And they don't want to know the truth.
CHRISTOPHER:	Some of that is your own fault. You set yourself up to be idolized by faking it and not telling people how hard life really is for you.
CHRIS:	Come on! We would not have made it this far, if I didn't grit my teeth, smile and pushed through it. They're not in my body feeling what it's like to have to fight against yourself. They have no idea what it's like to be diminished into a little boy and shoved into a corner just because of my physical limitation. And, they didn't ask. I just wanted to be accepted. I didn't think that they would put this type of expectation on me.
CHRISTOPHER:	But, Christian's expectations are not God's expectations. He doesn't expect you to live perfect in an imperfect world. He only expects you to do your best until He gets here or you get there. But you have fallen into the trap that the church has set for all people who want to believe in God. That trap is you can't make any mistakes. And you can't do anything outside of what they think is acceptable. You, like many, have let the church define your walk with Christ. And now here you are, ready to give in and throw in the towel, all because you are not living up to their expectations. Can I ask you a question? Where are they now? They are ashamed of you now. You have let them down so they believe you don't know God. Or they think God sees you the way they see you. They forget that God sees everyone through the sacrifice that Jesus made on the cross.
CHRIS:	I cannot be their hero. I'm just someone who decided to fight for a life. Now I'm going to be judged for

getting tired of being knocked down time and time again. I'm not Christ, but sometimes I think people expect me to bleed for them. They don't understand the bruises, cuts, and scrapes that this life has had on my soul. They don't realize that I can only take so many punches and knockdowns. They have taken the joy of being a Christian and turned it into an obligation I must fulfill.

CHRISTOPHER: Perhaps you were easily shoved into a corner because you wanted them to see you free instead of actually being free. There is something to say about fighting for someone else. There is even more to say when you are not willing to fight for yourself. So many people play basketball for their coach rather than for the enjoyment of the game. Yet they wonder why they feel so torn up when they make a foul play.

CHRIS: It's just that I know they don't expect me to deal with my pain and being abused. They don't expect me to have moments that I want to give up. It is hard living life with cerebral palsy. They don't expect me to have temptation and sin in my life. They don't expect me to deal with sexual thoughts. They expect me to be perfect because I'm a Christian.

CHRISTOPHER: You can't get back in the game for the wrong reason this time.

The Voice of Understanding: Christopher

I found myself being more of a Baptist than a Christian. Now before the Baptist preachers and the Baptist congregation get their feathers in a ruffle, let me clear up something. I believe this is true for all denominations. We sometimes get more caught up in the denomination rather than just trusting Him to lead us to the right church and the right body of believers. Here is my challenge to someone who is looking to get plugged into church: stop looking. You're not ready to go there. Here is what I suggest: Read the Bible from beginning to end. Based on the things that God reveals to you, find a church that lines up with what God has told you.

This is the hardest chapter for me to write. It still tears me up inside to think about and relive that time in my life. The thought of getting it published and letting the whole world know gives me a tight chest and butterflies in my stomach. I am ashamed of this more than anything else. So why am I continuing? Because I believe someone is going to benefit from me sharing my story.

I also believe that God will be glorified in the end.

I am surprised things went this far. There have always been moments in Chris' life when he thought about giving up or ending it. However, I was always able to convince him to keep going. But we never experienced as much adversity as we have experienced in the last couple of years. I knew it was taking a toll on us. To be truthful, I let down my guard. The situation was getting to me as well, and I allowed Chris to be overwhelmed by his emotions. I realized now as we were growing up, Chris was taking on the characteristics and mindset of the disabled label. The label brainwashed him into thinking that I, Christopher, could never exist according to society's standards, knowledge, and understanding.

The weird part of this whole situation is Chris did exactly what society expects him to do. The common consensus of society would say that there is no reason for someone with a severe disability to want to live. They will say they understand why Chris wanted to take his own life. That understanding comes out of a self-reflection. The truth is many people would attempt suicide if they had to deal with a sudden disability. Many individuals who lose their ability to completely function in society because of an accident become immediately depressed and have serious thoughts of suicide. The thought of living life insufficiently according to the world's standards overwhelms them, not to mention all the other things that Chris had to deal with beyond being a person with a disability.

So much has been stolen from me. From the time I was born, it seemed like this world has continued to try to decrease whatever worth I have. My father stole a chance from me to know what it is like to live in a home with two parents who care about each other and the well-being of their children. He also stole from me a chance not to live in poverty. Momma tried so hard to provide for us, and she did a good job at it, but she could only do so much. She definitely couldn't provide anymore than she did. Lee, her boyfriend, has stolen a lot from me as well. I will never know what it's like to grow up in a peaceful environment. I will always be looking over my back and be afraid of someone hurting me. I will always find it difficult to trust someone. Roy took away my sexual innocence. I think that was the most valuable thing I will ever own, and he took it away very early in my life. Though I understand sex and the way Christianity says it is supposed to be, I will forever be confused and sex will never be the way it could have been. The disabled label has robbed me of my self-esteem. My disability justifies society's tactic to treat me like I am less than the next person. Society has taken their fair share too. Society has made me feel like I can't be a part of it because of the disabled label. They tell me every day in some way, shape, or form that I should just sit at the window and watch the world go by because they don't want me to be part of what makes the world go round. And, finally, the church, all that they are worried about is seeing a miracle, not for my good, but for their faith. I'm just their guinea pig that they want to see healed. They are not helping me embrace who God made me to be.

It seems like everybody has taken a piece of my life. I am going to beat all of those who tried to beat me, who tried to take my life from me. I am going to beat them, not at their own game but at my game. My game is survival. My game is to be able to smile when it's all over. How am I going to accomplish this? By taking back everything they stole from me. I was too close to just giving up and giving them my whole life. I never thought that it was mine to take back. Now I realize it is mine, and I am going to live the life that God gave me by taking it back from the rest of the world.

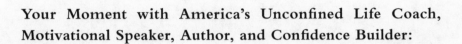

Your Moment with America's Unconfined Life Coach, Motivational Speaker, Author, and Confidence Builder:

Sometimes giving up is necessary to keep going. There are wrongs we can't make right. Therefore, the right thing for us to do is to accept what is wrong. Our inability to correct the issue can make us feel inadequate and cause us to give up on ourselves.

What things have you always believed about yourself?
Do you need to take something back that has been stolen from you?
Are you too close to giving up?

CHAPTER 19

Answer the Call, Regardless

The Voice of Experience: Chris

The society we live in is a malfunctioning machine that regulates the oxygen level for an individual who may or may not be capable of breathing on their own. It doesn't monitor the heart, mind, or soul. This machine takes the common census of all who appear to be in the same group. The census gives the machine justification for judging a book by its cover and therefore regulating the oxygen level for all in that group. The machine, society, has failed to see the malfunction of its approach. As a result, many people are not receiving the amount of oxygen that is needed for a full life. I want the opportunity to live.

I can breathe on my own, but my condition has forced me into a group called the disabled. All who are in this group must live on the machine. This machine regulates my oxygen. This machine, society, not only controls my breathing; it also confines me to a certain amount of space. This machine will not allow me to go any farther than where I am. I must sit in this spot, lie in this bed, and only move within these four walls. The longer I live on this machine, the closer I am to death. Let me breathe or let me die! But don't keep me here, reliant on the machine for survival! I want the opportunity to live.

Out of all my cousins, uncles, brothers, and sisters, I am the only college graduate in my whole family. I cannot deny I am proud of that. For my whole life, everyone has been telling me what I cannot do. They look at my wheelchair and minimize my capabilities to such a degree that I appear to be insufficient. However, in the fall of 1998, I received a bachelor of science degree in technical and professional communications from the university I attended. Only 13 percent of people with a disability twenty-five and older have a bachelor's degree or higher. This compares with 31 percent of those without a disability, according to the U.S Census Bureau.

At this point in my life, I feel like I am no longer physically confined, though I am still in the wheelchair and will always live my life with cerebral palsy. I am confident that I have proven my abilities to those around me. Now, just like most people, I have to break through personal, professional, spiritual, and financial barriers. Though they are the same barriers everyone has to break through, these barriers will be especially challenging for me. Even though I am not a prisoner in my own body anymore, I will always be viewed as someone who was incarcerated. I still have to live with the same unfair stigma as a person who was locked up. There will always be preconceived notions about my physical and mental abilities.

The next decade and a half of my life, I will be living in a society that will understand that I am different from them physically, but they will remain blinded from our personal, professional, spiritual, and financial similarities. Everyone understands that I have a heart, mind, and soul. Now I have to show them that I have rights, worldviews, and I am worthy of respect just like the next person. The stigma and preconceived notions of a person with a disability will force me to become an expert on breaking through physical, personal, professional, spiritual, and financial barriers.

My first barrier was financial. I wanted to be financially unconfined. To me, this is when a person's resources can sustain them and benefit others. I was a long way from this. Graduating at the top of my class looks good on paper, at least good enough to get a phone call to come in for an interview. But the minute they hear my voice, they hang up the phone or shut down the line of communication.

So far, I was able to go on three interviews because the invitation was given to me over e-mail. For every interview, I went in there wearing my best suit, with absolute confidence that I could do what they were asking me to do. But the moment they took one glance at me, their eyes glazed over, and I knew that I had no chance of communicating my ability to that individual. It didn't matter to them if I had enough ability to dedicate the last five years of my life to getting a degree. In their minds, I was incapable of doing the job. One lady even said to me in an interview, "Why are you wasting my time? You need to get back into your car now and go home. We are not hiring." Then she walked away. I found an interesting report by a Lou Harris poll. They said, "People with disabilities often encounter job discrimination. Two-thirds of people with disabilities who are of working age are not working, according to a Lou Harris poll. This high unemployment rate is not because people with disabilities don't want to work; two-thirds of those not presently working do want to work."

As they say, meanwhile back at the ranch, I am very involved in my single's group and loving church. God and I have got a good thing going on. I understand His sovereignty in my life now. I am even going around sharing my story in different Sunday school classes every Sunday. Some of the classes even take up money for me, which is helping me to support myself, as I figure out what I am going to do with my life. One night after coming home from church, I had another internal ego conflict.

CHRIS: I love sharing my testimony. I really think it is helping people.

CHRISTOPHER: This is what I am born to do.

CHRIST:	This is what I called you to do. This is the one thing that nobody can tell you "no" because I said "yes."
CHRIS:	No not me. You've got the wrong one, baby.
CHRISTOPHER:	You have already been doing this. Just make it official.
CHRIST:	Yeah you. This is what I called you to do.
CHRIS:	A small Sunday school class is nothing compared with a big church. Going from church to church, speaking in front of hundreds, maybe thousands of people. Not me, God.
CHRISTOPHER:	You are the one this time, saying, "You're not good enough."
CHRIST:	I've got a message for my people only you can deliver. And you are sufficient enough to deliver it. You're more than good enough. You're perfect for this.

A couple weeks later, I got a call from one of my closest college friends, asking me to come out and speak in front of his company out in California. He was even willing to pay me. At first, I was very, very hesitant; but I accepted the invitation. The company flew me out to Huntington Beach, California, to speak to their top salesmen from all over the United States. I can't tell you how nervous I was. However, I remember one lady walking into the room. When I started to speak, I could tell that she was depressed, angry, and mad at the whole world. I felt her defeat. In a way, I actually connected with her. I continued to speak, not really knowing what I was saying; however, tears started rolling down her face. By the end of whatever I said, don't ask me what it was, her whole demeanor changed. And in that moment, on that stage, I said to God, and myself "Yes."

That was Christopher that put his "yes" on the table, not Chris. I still struggle with my past and all the things I have done up until this point. By no way did I feel worthy of going into any type of ministry. Though I haven't acted on it, I still struggle with bisexual thoughts. I can hide my thoughts and desires from the outside world, but I cannot deny them to myself. If anyone found this out, I would be labeled as fallen from the ministry and no longer worthy of my calling. So once again, I got myself back into counseling.

Why did He call me to do this in the first place? He knows my background. He knows everything that I struggle with. He knows how the church will frown upon me if my struggles come out. I cannot admit to my struggles and temptations. How can I call myself a man of God with the past and the struggles that I deal with every day?

If I were truly honest with myself, I would have to admit that Jesus and I still have some issues. I don't struggle with the fact that I was born with cerebral palsy. I can deal with that. What I do struggle with are the things that happened in my childhood up until now that God could have prevented. I do not understand why I had to go through the painful experiences I went through. It's true some of the things I went through cannot be covered up. I am learning in counseling that it must be acknowledged and brought to the surface. People often become mentally and/or emotionally neuropathic. This is when a person mentally or emotionally becomes numb to the hurtful events that they experience in life. Honestly, I cannot list all of the events that have caused me pain and have torn down my self-esteem. Nor can I ignore the results of them.

Does God or man really expect me to go through all of these things and not be affected by them? The truth is I have some mixed thoughts and emotions. Many would say I have those thoughts because of what I went through. I do not know about all of that. I just know, I'm going to live life out of the pain of my experiences at some point. I'm going to ask why at some point. I'm going to be angry at some point. I have to be at peace with the fact that God cannot change what has happened, and He is not upset with me asking Him to help me understand. I don't care who it is; people's actions will always be based on their experiences and what they do and do not understand. If I know that, then I guarantee God knows it as well; hence grace, mercy and sovereignty.

Satan is certainly trying to use my speech impediment, my wheelchair, my past, my struggles, the label, society, and even the church to discourage me from doing what I know God wants me to do. "You should not be here. They will not understand you. You are not worthy enough to talk about the Lord. You are disabled and not as important as the next person. No one really loves you; they just tolerate you. You will never be good enough." I hear that over and over in my head every day. However because of grace, mercy and sovereignty, I am moving forward with what I know He called me to do.

When I first started speaking, I only shared the good things of my life. I did not want to share about the physical and emotional challenges I faced from day to day. I'm in pain every day of my life. Sometimes seizure after seizure gets the best of me. I get aggravated when I'm home alone, and I can't button up my shirt or tie my shoes, and sometimes it does tick me off when people in public look at me funny because I'm in a wheelchair, my body is all crooked, and my voice is not clear. They say, "The anchor holds, though the ship has been battered." I'm starting to understand that now.

As you can imagine, when I made it official and told people that I was called to become a keynote speaker, they were shocked and very discouraging. I heard over and over again, "Chris, you can't do that. They won't understand you. People are looking to hire good communicators. No offense, but with your voice, you cannot do it." And, frankly, I agreed with them. But we are not dealing with Chris. We are dealing with Christ and Christopher. When these two make up their minds, what they want to do, all I can do is take a seat in the back and hang on for the ride. Especially when it comes to Christopher, all I can do is shake my head. I am not going to try to tell him what he can't do. You can certainly try. Many people have. Very few people have won that argument.

The Voice of Understanding: Christopher

After putting my *yes* on the table, it was six months later when God made it very clear what my specific calling is. My purpose is to help all people understand that real joy cannot be confined. It is not my goal to win or receive any type of sympathy or to make people feel guilty. My purpose is to simply say, "If I, in the midst of all my trials, tribulations, and cerebral palsy, can live an unconfined life, then what possible reason could you have not to?" My calling is to motivate, challenge, and encourage people to stop living their lives confined to what I call a "wheelchair."

I'm not what some may call an evangelist. I feel my role as a speaker is to use my life experience, knowledge, and love to motivate, encourage, and challenge people to break free and find victory, freedom, joy, peace, and love. Therefore, I do not seek out to speak only on spiritual platforms.

Some people say I have a magnetic personality. People feel drawn to me. That may be true, but I just enjoy doing what I do. I especially love cutting up with the audience, making them laugh, and saying some things that they would never think a person in my situation would lighten up and say. Every now and then, I intentionally put them in an awkward position. One of the favorite things I like to do is call someone out when I know they are pretending to understand what I am saying. This makes for a good icebreaker, and people start to realize that I am human, just like they are. Not only that, but I am getting comfortable with who I am and allowing my sense of humor to blossom.

For example, the other day, a friend of mine and I were walking in the hall after church. An elderly lady who recognized my friend, came over to us and asked, "Who is your special friend?" Before my friend could reply, I did by saying, "This is Mitch." The stunned and confused look on her face could best be described by an American Express commercial, "Priceless."

I believe that my joy, through my suffering, is playing a very vital role in my career and personal relationships. Even though I have my physical and emotional ups and downs, I believe the love, joy, and peace I have deep within rises to the surface when I am on stage. I believe this joy is the magnet that draws people to me. When I have the opportunity, it is a privilege to be able to say it's my Lord in me that you are drawn to.

I believe that God has me on earth simply for the people in my life. I believe He wants to use me to show them someone that they see as less fortunate but has found real joy in the midst of his circumstances. I know my life is a challenge to people. When the joy comes out in my smile, people have to ask themselves questions like, "Why am I down or discouraged? What am I complaining about?"

People that live their lives without purpose are living a confined life. The question, "Why me?" must be answered for everyone. Too many people are living life without a passion. They don't have a reason to fight back. The unanswered question "why?" has left them empty inside.

I'm not empty. I'm full now because at the end of the day regardless of the labels, regardless of the stereotypes that come with the labels, regardless of what society says I am or am not good for, regardless of what the church considers to be a whole and healed person in Christ, and regardless of my internal struggles, I have a passion. I know why I am suffering, and the suffering is worth the outcome. Knowing why is the foundation to living an unconfined life. This is the beginning of pursuing a life that is no longer confined.

<hr />

Your Moment with America's Unconfined Life Coach, Motivational Speaker, Author, and Confidence Builder:

The word "regardless" is one of the most powerful words in life. This word cuts the crap out of our lives and forces us to see what is in front of us. Regardless of their past, everyone must come out of their emotional and spiritual rut.

What should you be doing with your life regardless of what you are doing now?

Are you allowing a person to define your self-worth and tell you what you can and cannot bring to this life, regardless of what you know and believe?

Regardless of your past, are you living in faith, grace, and mercy? Do not forget He is sovereign.

CHAPTER 20

The Crossroads of Life

The Voice of Experience: Chris

I was dating someone again. My favorite thing was when I would be at the table or the desk doing something, and she would walk up behind me, put her arms over my shoulder, and begin to help me in whatever I was doing. It felt like she was a part of me. I never knew what it felt like to be so close to someone. This was my first time since college that I have had a Christian relationship. I loved having her hair in my face. I loved knowing that someone that wanted to be there was beside me. It wasn't my family. It was someone who had chosen to be a part of my life and embraced me.

But I sensed that she was ashamed of our relationship. When we were around our mutual friends and in church, she pretended like we were just good friends. She didn't touch me at all or give me any type of attention that would let someone know. Everybody could see that there was something more going on, even though she was trying hard not to reveal it. I was OK with dating her; however, Christopher was not. He feels like she thought she was too good for him. According to Christopher, she is insecure with her own self and therefore will never be secure with dating a

157

man like him. So he broke it off with her. I'm not sure he did the right thing.

One day, the church staff and I went out for lunch. During lunch, I needed to go to a restroom that was not set up for someone with a disability. As a result, I slipped, fell, hit my head, and went into multiple seizures. Because of this, I started to suffer short-term memory loss. When I arrived at the emergency room, my father, with whom I had little to no communication with my whole life, arrived in Atlanta. My mom, back in Baton Rouge, called him to ask if he could just go check on me until she got there. He arrived sometime that day after they put me in a private room and drugged me up very well. Like I said, I had lost my short-term memory; but for some reason, when he entered my room, I must have remembered the pain that he had caused me. I cannot tell you exactly what I said, but my coworker who was with me said I laid into him so heavily that he started to cry. My coworker also said I told my father, "This friend, who has only known me for two years, has more love for me than my own father." This pain that I had in my heart for twenty-seven years had to be released.

He never retaliated for what I said to him. His reply, or lack of reply, played a very crucial role in my life since then. My healing came when he gave me the medicine of acceptance. Maybe what I wanted all those years was for him to accept the pain that he caused me. That made all the difference in the world. We don't have the best relationship; however, I can respect him for allowing me to express the pain that he caused me rather than denying it. Things are not perfect now between us. But every day it grows closer and closer because I am choosing to let go of the past. I realize that it did not matter if he was right or wrong.

I know that I can go home at any time I want and my basic needs will be taken care of for the rest of my life. Momma will always provide me with a warm place to lay my head and food to eat. But just as always, I know I can do more with my life. So I have been hanging in there, and it has been a slow process, but we are getting there. I will not quit because I know this is my calling, and God wants to do something great through my life.

I find myself financially confined a lot. Many months I go without getting paid from the nonprofit organization, because it just can't afford it. Running a nonprofit organization means relying on contributions from individuals to support your cause and what you want to accomplish. It's true the organization gets paid for me to speak to other organizations. The reality is it requires much more financial support than a speaking opportunity once or twice a month. This is why support is so very important.

I am so tired of receiving government benefits. I know I can do so much more with my education than to rely on a social program to take care of me. I have been going through a vocational agency funded by the government to help people with disabilities find jobs in the workplace. The counselor was looking for a job that I can do, making $400 to $500 a month, and still receive my benefits rather than helping me find a career that I can one day live independently of my social benefits. To be frank, this surprises me. I thought that someone that works in the field of helping disabled people succeed would be much more encouraging than she was. But instead, she was more discouraging to me. She too wanted to confine me to society's thought of a person with a disability. So here I am at this vocational crossroads. Do I just do enough to supplement my government assistance, or do I step out there and continue my career in hopes that one day it will allow me to be free from government programs?

You will find a group of people in the world who will say, "It's OK. That's what government programs are for. Being black and disabled gives you the right to be on social security and welfare." Lou Harris reports that there is a staggering unemployment rate that does not stem from the lack of desire to work. Two-thirds of people with disabilities want to be working. The study also shows that people with disabilities perform as well or better than their coworkers. According to an ADA committee report, you will find that 18.2 million people with disabilities want to work. And over 20 percent of those people are living in poverty. People with disabilities have more than twice as high of a poverty rate as other Americans. I don't want to be in those statistics.

I will not remain financially confined. Being unconfined financially is a mindset. It is not about how much money you have; it's about knowing you earned what you have. I understand that there are some people that are in situations that make it difficult for them to provide their basic needs. I am not convinced I am one of these individuals. I am not about to use my race nor disability as an excuse not to provide for myself. Too many people give into the stereotype that society places on them. We think that if society tells us that we are thugs, then we act like thugs; or if society tells us we are black, we act in whatever it means to act black, Mexican, or Indian. In other words, I am not going to be confined to society's thoughts about me.

I met another girl, while speaking, that I really like a lot. Julia has cerebral palsy as well. Not half as severe as mine, her voice is clear, and she is able to walk on crutches while dragging her feet around. She is very educated and well accomplished. I never thought I would meet someone with cerebral palsy who is just as ambitious as I am. Julia is very determined to have a successful life regardless of her physical condition and what the world thinks of it. It's also nice to be in a relationship with someone who understands the social complications and, physical and emotional struggles that come with having this condition. It took me exactly eighteen hours to track her down, give her a call, and ask her out on a date. The first thing she asked was how old I am. After convincing her that I was older, she agreed to go out with me. However, there were some issues. One is neither one of us can drive. She lives in the city of Atlanta, while I live on the outskirts of Atlanta, at least twenty minutes away; but the attraction was strong enough for the both of us to find a way to see each other.

She is overly aggressive and very easily offended. Her passion to better the lives of people with disabilities is often expressed in anger and threats. She is one that will tell you it's wrong to call someone handicapped; you should call them disabled. If you call someone disabled, you are wrong, and you should say physically challenged. And if you say physically challenged, why must you label them at all? I say to her many times, "What does it matter? You have cerebral palsy no matter how you spin it." This causes a major argument between us. Having arguments is a routine for us. When I am with her, at some point in our time together, we will disagree.

I knew our relationship was going to cause more strife and difficulties than I was prepared to deal with. But a part of me wanted it to work. I told myself all the time, "What if she is the only girl that would possibly marry me?" Because of cerebral palsy, she understands me more than any other girl I have dated in the past. But I knew it would not work out. When a person holds on to their ideal situations in a perfect ideal world those situations have a stronger grip on them than they have on the situations. In order to live personally unconfined, life a person must let

go of the things that have a grip on them. When I released all I was trying to hold on to I was personally set free.

What are the definitions of failure and success? Am I a failure? Am I a failure because I cannot physically do what the next man can? Am I a failure because I do not have a white picket fence, a dog, two kids, a trophy wife, a mistress on the side, and a one-hundred-twenty-hour job a week to support all of it? Am I a failure because I understand that I am weak and therefore cannot be my own God? Am I a failure because I do not have the time for shallow conversations or to chase temporary fixes?

According to society, the answer to this question is yes. I am a failure because of all of the above. But there is one thing that I will say I am successful in, and that is my ability to sit back in a corner and analyze the situation. After analyzing society's answer to my question, I have concluded that the only thing I fail at is conforming to society's definition of success. I have failed to live up the expectations of a materialistic and shallow society. I am a failure because I chose to live my life not afraid of the stigma of a ridiculous stereotype.

I have successfully failed to fall into society's trap. I refused to be confined by my situation, be defined by money, and be denied by individuals who try to live up to society's definition of success. I am successful because I have embraced my limitations and used them to expose my strengths. I am successful because I found the fine line between appreciating and idolizing the finer things in life.

There are many who wake up every day, put on the masquerade, run the rat race, and climb the corporate ladder only to look back at me in envy of the simplicity of my life. In that moment when our eyes meet, while they are hanging on to the corporate ladder for dear life and I am sitting in the wheelchair enjoying life; we both realize that society has failed us. Society has given them the wrong definition of failure and has given me the wrong definition of success. We could debate on who has the better perspective at this point, but they are too busy trying to avoid failure, and I am too busy enjoying my success.

Speaking of crossroads in your life, the other day, I was on my way to a singles Bible study with some friends of mine. It was a day I will never forget. My van was loaded with five other people and my wheelchair. We were having a great time just talking, laughing, and looking forward to the events of the night. My Motorola phone beeped at me to notify me that my brother Dewayne was trying to get a hold of me. I clicked the button that allowed me to talk to him. I said, "What's up?"

DEWAYNE: Paul is dead.
CHRIS: I can't hear you. What did you say?
DEWAYNE: Your brother Paul is dead.

For some reason, my ears were not allowing me to comprehend what he was saying. I quickly passed my phone to the person sitting next to me and asked them to interpret what Dewayne was saying. My brain and heart weren't accepting what my ears were hearing. Then I heard once more: my hero, father, and best friend was dead. The only person that truly believed in me regardless of what I was trying to accomplish was dead. I started to hyperventilate and asked them to pull over in a shopping center parking lot so I could get some air. It seemed like everything was closing in on me. I remember asking God, "How much more are You going to give me?"

I knew going into the funeral, my family expected me to be an unemotional robot that can sit in front of a casket where his dead brother lies. I tried to, but I couldn't. No one knows the conversations we had. No one knows how much he gave to me even when he was down and out. No one knows the very day before he died, we had a four-hour conversation, and we ended with I love you. All my emotions, everything that was bothering me with this whole family, made me blow up. Before I knew it, I was wiped out of the sanctuary into the hall where my brother Lamont was adamantly telling me to stop crying. I asked him, "What right do you have to tell me to stop crying? I have a right to grieve too." My family didn't even acknowledge what I was trying to express. All that they thought was that I was drawing more attention on the situation by letting people see how weak and vulnerable I am.

The pain that I was experiencing at that moment felt like something that I had never felt before. The abuse, the heartache, the rejection, and every bit of confusion that I had ever experienced in my life were nothing in comparison with the pain I had then. It felt like my heart was frozen down to the core, and only that last layer was still beating. But don't get me wrong. It was beating through layers and layers of frozen flesh. I felt like it was stuck, wanting to beat completely but only beating just enough to keep me alive. I can't help but ask God what He is doing in my life. Why has He taken

Paul away from me? Like anyone, the pain of losing someone dearly to you brings you to a crossroads with your spiritual beliefs.

At that crossroad, God knew I was ready to become a conqueror. I love Paul, and I thank God for allowing Paul to be my backbone for so long. Now I know life is not just about surviving. It is about conquering. I needed Paul to survive; I needed faith in God and myself to conquer life. Losing Paul was a test of my belief, love, and faith.

Your Moment with America's Unconfined Life Coach, Motivational Speaker, Author, and Confidence Builder:

Our belief, love, and faith will eventually be put to the test. The bottom line question will always be "What direction your belief, love, and faith will lead you in."

Are you at a crossroad?

What do you see ahead in each direction?

What are the pros and cons of going in one direction and not the other?

CHAPTER 21

Racially Unconfined

The Voice of Understanding: Christopher

I believe that everyone has an overarching mission in life. This mission shall always remain in the forefront of our minds, but within that overarching mission, I believe we each have background missions. Small things that we all can accomplish and do along the way of achieving our ultimate goals in life. One of my background missions is to prove to my family and to the black culture that the world is changing, and even though we live in the South, there are still good, decent, honest Caucasians. No doubt about it; there were incidents in my life that has made this a very difficult mission.

Raised up by a black family and living the last half of my life in a predominately white society has given me the opportunity to see both sides. You can say that I was raised up on both sides of the tracks. To be honest with you, both sides have some things wrong and some things right. There are good things on both sides and evil things on both sides. I have met some prejudiced white people as well as some prejudiced black people. Both sides tried hard to play a role in keeping me racially confined. Don't think I'm trying to play the race card. Race is not a game that I play; it is an issue that I have to confront. The fact is I live in a part of the country where bigotry, a lack of understanding, and hate are covered up. I am no fool. Life in the South educates anyone who pays attention. The South, even with the large Christian churches on every corner, is still segregated. It was heartbreaking for me, but one of the hardest lessons I had to learn is being a Christian doesn't necessarily mean that person is not racially confined.

My family often hints around about their dislike of the fact that most of my friends are white. They often say to me, "Don't forget what color you are." Of all of the statements that burn me up the most, this is the one that pushes my buttons to no end. For several reasons. First of all, how could I ever forget what color I am? I wake up every day black. That's like me forgetting I am disabled. There is no way around that. Not that I want to wake up any other color than black. I am proud of my heritage, and I am proud of where we are as a society today as black Americans.

Yes, I say black Americans. I don't believe in labeling myself African American. I am an American. I am from America. I feel like African American is just another way of segregating myself from the rest of America. Another thing that burns me up about the saying *don't forget what color you are*, is the fact that I have spent my whole life trying not to be confined by my disability, and now culture and my family is trying to confine me to my color. Race is definitely a stronghold in America. People have used racism as a tool to define and confine themselves as well as other people. Who has time for the ridiculous method of allowing people in and out of their lives based on color? A racially unconfined person looks at the character of each individual and then makes their decision based on that.

I'll be the first to admit that I have my fair share of black-and-white jokes. In fact, a buddy of mine and I intentionally called each other by a racist name in order to get a response out of those around us. "What's up, my nig," he would say. Everyone's eyes got so big as they waited for my response. After a few seconds, I would reply by saying, "What up, you poor white trash?" The silence would then transform into a loud room of laughter.

Then there was a white girl in my circle of friends I was close with. Everyone in the group used to say that we had a thing for each other. We loved each other as a person but not romantically. She was easy to embarrass. So for her fortieth birthday party, I decided to play a little joke on her. I brought a fake engagement ring and presented it to her in front of everybody at this party. She turned red. She wanted to laugh, but because we were so close and I played it so well, she did not know how to reply. At that point, I decided to really embarrass her in front of everyone by asking her if was she turning down my proposal because I was disabled or black. Everyone laughed hysterically.

I have to admit sometimes I feel like I am some people's token black friend, and the fact that I am disabled just looks even better in the public eye or vice versa. I am their token disabled friend who happens to be also black. It bothers me to know I am the only black friend most of them have. I wonder if some people are my friend because I am a disabled man in spite of the fact that I am black. Some would say, "No, it's because you are a Christian." However, I am not the only black Christian in this world. I don't mean to be cynical, but you can see how this would be a thought in the back of my mind. I also know I have been given opportunities because of sympathetic people who see my physical condition and are blinded to the color of my skin.

I have tried to indirectly challenge several of them on this issue. You probably can imagine the different responses I have gotten. My favorite has been, "You don't really act black." My thoughts on this statement were *how do you act black*. What stereotype have they placed on black people that I don't fit into? Never once have I denied the fact that I am black. Everyone knows I love the black culture: our music, our food, our humor, and our style of clothes. The statement, "You don't act black," comes from a mind-set that has been defined and confined by the media. I am beginning to think that some people are not necessarily narrow-minded, their minds has been constrained by the people and things that they chose to allow to shape who they are. Now to be honest, even I have to be careful not to fall into the same trap. Sometimes I want to slip into their confined mind-set and respond by saying, "You don't act like poor white trash, but what does that have to do with it?"

I am aware that some people in my culture and family will think that me choosing to remain in this environment makes me a modern-day Uncle Tom. If I'm not careful, the term "Uncle Tom" can become just another stereotype to make me racially confined. As leader of the unconfined life movement, I am here to help people move beyond the stereotypes and racial barriers that have confined this country for so long.

But I am not blinded nor am I ignoring the racial barriers this country still has to break through. For instance, by going to an all white church, I have put myself in a vulnerable position. I did not realize this until the election between Barack Obama and John McCain. That turned out to be a very interesting time for me. Many of my friends tried to beat around the bush in order to find out my perspective on Obama's presidency. "So what do you think about McCain? Seems like a solid guy, don't you think? These are the many reasons why I would not vote for Obama," many have said to me. Then my favorite, "He is the Antichrist." Really, Christians? Is that what the Bible says the Antichrist would be like? Of course, of all the places in the world, the Antichrist is going to show up in our precious country first and be black. Why would the Antichrist not be black? Jesus was white according to the pictures I have seen.

I immediately felt my friendships were now being put to the test. I felt like they were trying to figure out if I have the same views that they think every other black person in America has. And if I did, I would no longer be worthy of being a friend of theirs. These friends were judging my character based on my political views. I would go so far as to say for a brief moment, those who did know my political views no longer saw me as a "brother in Christ." They chose to forget that there were just as many white American Christians as black American Christians who believed in Obama's ability to run this country.

Like I have already mentioned, some have said regardless of the fact that Obama is black, he is the Antichrist, and his political views will destroy this country. Three and a half years later, I have to bring their point back to the surface. Because then we had Mitt Romney running for president. Mitt Romney is a known Mormon. There was no guessing his religious beliefs. We didn't have to fabricate or come up with some notion that he may not believe in the same God we evangelical Christians believe in. However, there are many evangelical Christians that were behind this candidate who also supported the ridiculous notion that Obama may be the Antichrist and therefore should not be elected as president of this country. One person even told me that they do not care what his religious beliefs are as long as he gets this country "back where it needs to be financially." And this was the same person that stressed to me the importance of having a president with Christian values and standards.

Another upsetting thing to me is how many Christian institutions backpedaled on the separation of church and state during this time. For instance, back in May of 2010, a university that is known to train and equip young Christians to be strong believers in their work and community, actually allowed Glenn Beck, who is a political radio personality and also a Mormon, to give the commencement speech at the graduation ceremony. Then in 2012, that same university turned around and invited Mitt Romney to speak at their graduation ceremony. Things like this make me wish that I could somehow live out my faith in God without being called a Christian. I am not and will never be ashamed of Christ. However, the actions and the perspectives of some Christians are contradictory to the teachings of Jesus.

After working in a predominately white church for many years, I have found many churches have a Spanish ministry, Asian ministry, singles ministry, high school ministry, middle-school ministry, food ministry, and homeless ministry. You will not find a predominantly white church dedicated to ministering to the black community. I remember so many times going out and evangelizing with members of my previous church. No matter where we were or how many black people were in the area, the group would always go up to those who are white, Hispanic, or Asian. Why not? We have a ministry and a program for them. Several times I challenged the group to go up to a group of black individuals. Once or twice, they said because I was with them, they felt it was OK to do so. This leads me to believe that if I wasn't with them, they would have never taken on my challenge.

The reality that Sundays are the most segregated and judgmental day of the week in our whole country vexes me to no end. What is this that we can work among one another, live around one another, play sports with one another, but can't worship with one another? The church has been leaders in so many social issues other than reconciliation between races. I strongly feel that God is very disappointed with this fact. For the church not to be leaders in racial reconciliation says that we have not gotten the foundation of Christianity right. We can raise our voice and protest about abortion and prayer in schools, which are important. However, the basic principle that God wants us to exercise is love and unity among all cultures and race. Let me be clear: when I talk about discrimination, I am not just talking about the white church. I'm also talking about blacks, Hispanics, and Asians who only reach out to their community when God has made it very clear that all are equal.

Like I said in the beginning of the chapter, proving to the black culture and my family that things are changing is difficult but not impossible. I do have some very close and dear friends that are white. I would not trade them for anything. Their contribution to my life has been vital. I would like to believe that those friends know who they are and are secure enough with our friendship to see the benefits of me addressing this issue. I am totally confident that I have some great friends who have gotten past my race as well as my disability. They are not only racially unconfined but they have also played a role in helping me to continue to be unconfined in this area as well. Being a disabled person, I need a lot of help to do the things I need to do in life. The good part about this is quickly becoming aware of who your true friends are and who are not. The friends who have stood by my side financially, professionally, spiritually, physically, as well as racially had to be in it for the long haul. Regardless of what I've been told about the white society, I cannot be blinded by the people who have embraced me as a family member and loved me unconditionally. In my book, in this book, you cannot see an individual as a charity case when you have allowed them to live life with you. These are the people that I wish to expose to the black culture and my family. These individuals in my life, who happen to be white, have the unconfined mind-set that I personally believe we all should have.

⇒◆⇐

Your Moment with America's Unconfined Life Coach, Motivational Speaker, Author, and Confidence Builder:

An unconfined person does not allow the physical appearance of another person to stop them from getting to know and appreciate that person. We miss out on the opportunity to love, grow, and be educated when we confine our mindset to what we see on television or through what we see in the media.

How many friends do you have that are of a different race?
Are you afraid or do you shy away from getting to know a disabled person?
Have you ever let preconceived notions and a confined mindset racially confine you?

CHAPTER 22

Standing Up in a Wheelchair

The Voice of Experience: Chris

A man with no direction may appear to be free but will always walk in someone else's boundaries. Everyone must solidify who they are, why they are who they are, and what changes they are willing to make to be free. Real freedom is reaching the point in life that one never lets go of the truth, regardless of the circumstances.

Christopher is dragging me through this thing he calls life. He doesn't realize that I am tired and worn out. To me, it doesn't matter what we accomplish or how much education we have. People will always belittle us. Why is he fighting so hard to take two steps forward when he knows we are going to be slapped back down and pushed into a corner? Our effort to pursue an unconfined life has not been easy on us. It has pushed us down, knocked us around, and tossed us back and forth. Maybe a life of freedom is just not meant for us.

There are many people who would say that I do not have a right, my worldview is useless, and my perspective should not be taken into consideration. We are living in a country that still does not fully understand or embrace an individual of a different race or a person with a disability. Even though people see how well dressed, educated, and accomplished I am, they immediately become blinded by the wheelchair that mobilizes my body. I believe, based on my experience, individuals with disabilities, black or white, male or female, are still the most segregated population in the whole country.

Some may be saying, "Come on. Is it that bad?" OK, let's start first thinking about the child that gets spanked for staring at me because of his curiosity rather than the parents taking time out to help their children understand what a disability is. How about the waiter that sees me engaging in a conversation with the rest of my friends at the table and then comes over and asks one of them what I want to drink or eat? It's a challenge for me when I know I have more education than the person that is talking to me as if I am an idiot. In my opinion, all of this is the collective ignorance of society.

CHRISTOPHER: What are you talking about? Why are you bringing all this stuff up?

CHRIS: You act like nothing ever happens. You just want to go on with your life, smile, and pretend that everything is OK when it is not.

CHRISTOPHER: It's not that I am pretending that everything is fine. I am trying to fight through it and get some purpose and meaning behind the life that I have been given.

CHRIS: I don't buy that purpose and meaning crap. The truth is you are trying to pretend it doesn't affect you. Remember what you used to say back in the day, "Fake it till you make it." I know it affects you because I am here. Remember me, Chris?

CHRISTOPHER: I remember you. I remember you well. I know you are here. You constantly let the disable label define you. You are the one that allows society to decide whether you are going to enjoy your life or not. You are the one that is looking for approval from the people in the church when you got it from God. You are an immature, insecure, hopeless boy. And oh, by the way, I don't have to fake it till I make it anymore. I have made it. Why can't you acknowledge that?

CHRIS: You want to talk to me about acknowledging something? I will acknowledge you have made it when you acknowledge that the world will never acknowledge you. You only have the acknowledgement you have made up in your mind and little world. Acknowledge that!

CHRISTOPHER: Why? To give you another reason to complain and give up? You do a good job of finding those reasons on your own.

CHRIS: OK. It is about time you tell me what you really feel. You don't like me very much, do you?

CHRISTOPHER: I hate when people call me by your name! No, I don't like you. I can't like you. You won't allow me to. Remember, I am a part of you. So if you don't like yourself, how can I like you?

The Voice of Understanding: Christopher

I had psychomotor agitation. This is psychological and physical restlessness. After all I had achieved, I still had a desire for peace with the things in life I could not escape. I had to deal with the fragile place in my life, the spot where my heart, mind, and soul separated because of the reality of life even after reaching what we call the top. I must tell you that my life is difficult and always will be because of my disability and the struggles that come with it. Dealing with psychomotor agitation forced Chris to break through barriers in his life.

I'm so proud of Chris. He is finally getting the guts to verbalize what he believes and question what he doubts. Though he is getting tired and weak because of the life that we have lived, his fragileness is forcing him to direct his energy toward important issues and life-changing decisions. Chris and I are beginning to experience a personal breakthrough.

I hate to admit it, but Chris is right. I tried to pretend that things don't bother me. But I am so sick of how society treated me just because I was in a wheelchair. I realized that even though I a am well educated and accomplished, I still have to deal with the image that most people have of a person with a severe disability, but I have to do it cleverly. I cannot just be a "bull in the china shop." Somehow I've got to draw the line between being cordial and not letting people treat me as if I am an uneducated invalid. I cannot ignore that society tends to belittle a person with a disability. As a thirty-eight-year-old man, I cannot tell you how tired I am of people who don't know me, calling me buddy. I can tell by their tone they are talking to me as if I am five years old. I think to myself, *You are definitely not smarter than a fifth grader.*

I have friends that have known me for years and still have moments where they respond to me according to what is ingrained in their heads rather than one of their peers. I know this to be true when I make a decision that they would not have made. And at that time, at that moment, they do not confront me as a peer that they want to give advice to; instead, they unconsciously speak to me as a teenager or a child that they must instruct. I think they feel, in spite of my age, intelligence, and free will, it is OK to express their concern and correct me in what I am doing. For example, a friend of mine came to pick me up at the airport. As usual, we decided to meet at the curb. I always have an airport employee take me from the gate to the pick-up spot. On the way, I tipped the person that was assisting me. Once I got to the car, my friend asked me if I tipped this individual. I told him I did, and everything was taken care of. Yet, and still, this friend chose to go into my wallet and pull out an additional two dollars to give to the individual who was helping me.

This communicated to me that my friend thought that whatever tip I did give was not good enough, and he had the authority to go into my wallet and give out additional tips. I firmly do not believe that my friend would go into anyone else's wallet and give an additional tip on someone else's behalf.

For a while, I did not vote, simply because freedom dictated by the perspective of another is not freedom. It's simply allowing a dog to run on a leash that you have control of. I do have an opinion on whom our officials need to be along with political views to back up my opinion. My right to vote was indirectly stolen from me because of my physical dependence on someone else to mark or circle the ballot for me. One time I went to vote, I was with a friend of mine who had in his mind that the candidates that I wanted to vote for were clearly the same candidates that he wanted to vote for. And so when it came down to marking the ballot, he placed his finger on his choice before I could verbally say who I wanted to vote for. He just waited for me to give him a signal to verify. Right then, my right to vote was stolen from me. I was immediately put in a position that no other "able citizen" in America is put into when it comes to elections. I had to defend my freedom to vote right there in the election booth or go along with his political views. It really bothered me that this friend that I trusted to take me to experience such a private right was treating me like it was OK to invade my beliefs. Unfortunately, I was more consumed by my hurt and disappointment than I was about defending my political views.

I have spoken in churches all over America for the past eleven years, received a certification on church planting and growth, as well as worked on the staff of two very large Baptist churches in the South. The church issues have appeared on my professional desk many times over the years. A friend of mine, who is very aware of my experience, agreed to look over this book. When they read my views on the church, she made it a point to write me a note. In summary, the note said that I did not have the experience to write what I just wrote.

Now I understand that they had the right to disagree with my view. However, there is a bigger issue here. If I was just another friend of theirs in ministry—walking, talking, and doing the things that they perceive as normal—they might not have challenged this at all. If they did, they would have probably challenged it in a different way. They might have said, "That is your opinion. I don't agree with it. You might want to approach it in a different way, or here's another perspective on this issue." But they would have never told that person with the same experience he was unqualified to make that statement. It appeared to me that they were confining my experience to their views of someone with a disability.

I don't think my friends realize what they are doing until I reply by saying, "Thank you, Mom or Dad." Sometimes I just have to remind them that I am a grown-ass man and I know what I am doing. Of course, I do it delicately. And right now, as I write this, I am thinking of some friends of mine that are not going to like this too well. Even though they know it is the truth, they think a person with a disability should not boldly declare their independence. What's the definition of slavery? Is it denying an individual to become their own person and declare the freedom that their country gives to all women and men? If so, can you understand now why I feel like I was born a prisoner?

Now please understand me. I do make mistakes. I need help and guidance and look forward to having wise people in my life to lead me the right way. However, when they tell me to do something that they would not tell the next man, I can't help but to think that they feel my disability has given them the liberty to treat me as if I am one of their children. The most effective way I have found to break through this barrier is to wait for the opportunity to use my wisdom to help them solve a problem that has occurred in their life. At that time, I found that my friends realize that I can not only make decisions but also bring something to the tables of their lives as well.

Recently, I decided to become a certified life coach. I enjoy coaching others on how to achieve their goals in life. After a couple of months of trying to figure out what would be the best institution to get my certification through, I decided on an institute based in California. I did all of my registration and the preliminary work for the course. About two weeks before the course started, while I was in Kansas giving a speech, I received a phone call from the founder and director of the program. She communicated to me that she was not allowing me to take her course based on the fact that she felt that I would slow it down and would not be able to keep up with her one-week training. I proceeded to explain to her that I have a college education, ten years in public speaking, ten years of running a nonprofit organization, a certification in human behavior, certification in church planting, and have written and published a book.

CHRISTOPHER: I assure you I can keep up with your course.
CHRIS: That won't matter to her. You are still disabled.
THE LADY: I went to your website, and I saw all of the things
                that you are doing. I am very proud of you, but I
                am still concerned that you will not be able to keep
                up with this intense training and don't want you to
                slow down the progress of the other students.

Now, in a perfect Christian world, perhaps I should have said, "God bless her soul. I hope she repents and changes her ways." But that was not my response when I hung up the phone. Frankly, I said to myself, *What a bitch!* Yes, I am a speaker who believes I should be careful of the terminology I use around certain people in certain arenas. I am trying to be transparent with you. There are moments that the best adjective to describe a person's character is the word "bitch." This was one of those times.

    She may not have known the correct terminology for what she was doing to me but in my eyes she was professionally confining me. Not allowing my education, background and experiences to continue to grow would have been forcing me to remain in the corner that many people put me in during the course of my life. To be professionally unconfined, one must always continue their education and find new avenues to display their education, background and experience. Therefore, within minutes of hanging up with her, I was on the phone with a lawyer, asking for representation. It took a couple of weeks of me not backing down and threatening to sue her institution before she finally gave in and allowed me to take her course. This is just one example of many incidents I have experienced and will continue to experience for the rest of my life regardless of my education, background, and experience. Many people will try to justify the behavior of her and other people I have spoken of in this book. Regardless of whatever excuses they come up with, the truth is for anyone to ignore another person's background, education, and experience because of their race, disability, or sexual preference is prejudice and confining in its purest form of the term.

I believe there comes a certain age in everyone's life when he or she no longer tolerates the things they used to. There are some things that we put up with as a child, teenager, or even a young adult, even though we don't necessarily agree with them. We feel the most respectful thing that we can do is to deal with it. Then after a certain age, you realize that you too deserve respect, respect for who you've become as well as where you are in life. At the age of thirty-eight, in spite of my disability, I have reached that point. I am no longer allowing people to talk to me, look at me, or treat me in a disrespectful way. I think many people, including some members of my family, feel that if a person has a disability, they should not reach that point in their life. They think a disability automatically disqualifies someone from the right of being respected as an adult. An ignorant person oftentimes tries to confine people around them to their limited knowledge. *No Longer Confined* is about declaring not only freedom but truth. The truth is regardless of my physical situation, I am a thirty-eight-year-old, disabled, accomplished, Christian black male who deserves to be treated with respect regardless of my wheelchair. Some people in my predicament will beg for this respect, jump through hoops, or hope that one day we will all become open minded, but not me. As of now, the respect that I deserve, I will expect of people. Anyone, from this point forward, friends and family who have an issue with this, will be dismissed from my life.

The freedom that I pursued all my life didn't come into fruition until I first defined who I was and my purpose. Now I have the boldness to help the world understand that I can see outside of the frame of my wheelchair. My disability does not give anyone excuses to devalue who I am.

———⟫◆⟪———

Your Moment with America's Unconfined Life Coach, Motivational Speaker, Author, and Confidence Builder:

A person must know who they are in spite of society. You must have a dialogue with yourself sometimes. It is these internal conflicts that help a person to come to grips with who they are, shape their worldview, and stand firm on their beliefs when they are questioned.

Does the reality of your life still agitate you?
What are you continuing to tolerate that you should not?
Have you confronted yourself?

CHAPTER 23

Pardon My French

The Voice of Understanding, Christopher

Someone recently asked me if I have any fears in life. From the age of fifteen until now, I have had two major fears. The first fear, if I'm truthful with myself, is obsolete. It is the fear of living my whole life confined to a wheelchair, mentally and spiritually. So many people in my predicament, along with many who don't have a physical disability, will never take the risk and challenges necessary to experience a full life. Their friends and loved ones around them also discourage them from doing so. Very early on in my life, I decided when I reach my deathbed I am not going to have the regret of not doing things I wanted to do just because of my disability. Now I will admit to you, because of that fear, I have put myself in danger. I have done some things that some people would say I shouldn't have ever done. But at the same time, at the age of thirty-eight, I can say that my life has been more fulfilled than people at the age of seventy without a disability. This fear that I have lived with enabled me to live a fulfilling life.

My second fear is what Redd Foxx says on Sanford and Son: "The big one." I am afraid that one day I will have a seizure that would put me back into a vegetative state. Truthfully, I do not want to live my life ever again confined to my body and absolutely relying on someone else for my every need. I have a fear of knowing what I know now and having that knowledge trapped inside of me. I know that the big one may never come. I can totally die of a car wreck or a heart attack, and I am OK with all of that. I just ask God not to put me back into that vegetative state where I have no control over my surroundings.

I have come to realize that freedom of speech is not just a right; it is a sign of life. To be able to express your thoughts, opinions, and feelings and know that someone has heard them and is responding to them is a sign that you are living. To know that you have been heard regardless of the response is something that I will never take for granted for the rest of my days.

Chris is dying. He doesn't have cancer or any type of terminal illness, but the life and the passion to live is being choked out of him daily. The disabled label, society, and the church is such a powerful combination that it is choking the life out of Chris. He is not strong enough to fight back. This combination would choke the life out of anyone. Every now and then, he comes up for air and contributes his two cents into the situation. For the most part, he's tired and doesn't want to exert his energy.

He had to tap out and allow me to get into the ring. Now don't get me wrong. I will make my mistakes. I would like to tell you from this point forward I was in control, and Chris quietly allowed the Christopher in him to come out, but that just wasn't the case. You see, I not only inherited Chris' fight against the disabled label, society, and the church; I also had to fight with Chris as well. There are moments in the midst of my insecurities when he creeps back up. There are times when society and the church forced him to rise to the surface and start a battle against me. We will always have arguments for the rest of our life, even though Chris is slowly dying.

The issue of healing has come up many times in my life. There are several incidents that come to mind. The first one is when I was much younger. I can't even recall the age that I was. But a person came up to me and alluded to the fact that if I just believe, if I had enough faith, that I would be healed. As a little boy not even eight years old yet, I had no idea what he was talking about. I know there are some kids that understand what faith is all about, but I did not have the understanding of who I was as a disabled child, and I certainly did not have an understanding of faith yet. To hear that God is keeping me in this situation because I do not have enough of something, even though I didn't understand what it was, hurt me. For a while, I was angry at God. I wanted to know what I was doing wrong to have Him terrorize me for this.

Another time I was faced with the healing issue was at a large Bible study in Alpharetta, Georgia. I was with a friend who remains to this day to be one of my best friends even though he was the vessel for the most embarrassing time in my life. The speaker started to speak on Mark, Chapter 2, where four guys took a paralytic up on a rooftop in order to lower him in front of the crowd and Jesus. My friend's interpretation of the speaker's message was that all people had to do was get their friends with disabilities to God in the same setting and they will be healed. So he interrupted the sermon and requested prayer over me, believing I could be healed that night. When he boldly and loudly made this request, I was immediately devastated and embarrassed. By the way, when I said a "large Bible study," I meant at least three to five thousand singles. There I was being put on the spot without any warning whatsoever. I truly wanted to crawl up under my wheelchair and die that night.

The speaker was put into a position where all he could do was stop his message and pray over me from a distance. His whole sermon was interrupted, and now he too was put on the spot as well. He prayed a very safe and generic prayer; however, those who attended this Bible study came from all walks of life, different denominations, and religious beliefs. Some of the people who laid their hands on me started praying things outside of the teacher's generic prayer, like, "release the demon out of his body" and "give him the faith to be healed." One gentleman proceeded to push me toward the end of my chair, trying to force me to my feet. At this point, I had to threaten him by saying, "If I fall and have a seizure, I'm suing you."

Needless to say, it was a quiet ride home, but please hear my heart. The friend who started this event is one of my best friends today. He was a young new Christian who did not understand the proper etiquette for an event like this. Today I am not mad at him. Embarrassed, yes, but not mad. I can even laugh about it now. But those who pray that the demons would leave my body or that I would have the faith to be healed, once again prove how the church needs to be careful with their interpretation of God's word and what it really means to be whole and healed as a Christian.

There was another time I ran into the issue of healing. Some friends of mine invited me to go eat with some other friends of theirs. These friends of theirs were very charismatic. In other words, they really believed that God wanted to heal anyone who believed they can be healed. While eating dinner, they looked over at me and said, "If you want to be healed, you can be healed." I knew where this was going. I tried to divert the conversation, but their minds were made up that they were going to see a healing that night, and I was the vessel for that healing or the guinea pig for their faith. Therefore, they pushed a little bit harder by saying, "You are not going to be healed because of your lack of faith." They knew that would push my buttons. They were saying that I am going to remain as I am because of my own actions. My own belief is the reason why I am in this wheelchair. Those words were a challenge to me.

I don't know if I did this to prove myself right or to prove them wrong, but I said, "OK, let's see." We went into the parking lot of

Fuddruckers in the middle of winter to prove what they believe or to confirm what I already accepted in my heart; God has a plan for me as I am. They said, "If you pray with me and believe in your prayers, you will get out of this chair and walk." So I prayed with them, knowing that God could do it but understanding that this very well could not be His will or timing for my life. Going into prayer, Chris showed up with a little bit of hope that they would prove me wrong. He wanted to believe that all of these years of working to accept my disability were contradictory to God's will for my life. Maybe God just wanted me to believe. So I prayed.

The next ten to fifteen minutes were filled with the group pulling me to my feet and watching me fall back into someone's arms time and time again. It seemed like every time I got up and fell, they backed up further away from me, hoping by doing this they would give me more time to catch my balance. After falling back into their arms time and time again, they finally gave up and said, "You just don't have enough faith. It's your own fault that you remain in the wheelchair."

Something in me began to well up inside, almost anger and rage. Because here is what I do know; It takes more faith for me to live my life in this wheelchair with peace, joy, and contentment than it does for me to hang on to the possibility of a miracle. I don't know how you measure faith. I don't know what amount of faith a person needs to be healed. But the Bible says: "It only takes the faith of a mustard seed to move a mountain." And I guarantee you I had more than that. God saw it fit not to heal me for whatever reason that night.

Whatever our situation may be, whether it is dealing with cancer, whether it is dealing with an illness or a disability, perhaps God wants us to get to the place in our lives where we are content. Whether He heals us or not, we have the joy of the Lord in our hearts. I will tell anybody, anywhere, anytime, yes, He will heal me. I don't know when that healing will come, but meanwhile, I have to live life in this chair. Now, today, I wonder if these people were struggling with their own lack of faith. What do I mean by that? Perhaps they didn't believe that God can give peace, joy, and contentment to a man who lives his life in a wheelchair.

Perhaps they thought, *Surely this person Christopher cannot be as content and happy as I am because he is not standing and walking and talking like I am.* Perhaps the real miracle of God is for a man to be in the middle of his adversities, in the middle of his challenges, and still have peace and joy. Now I tell you, not from faith, not from a belief, not from what I just read from the Bible, but from experience, this is possible. I don't have to hope for it. I got it. I got joy and peace and contentment. Yes, I am in a wheelchair. Yes, I am in pain. Yes, I struggle with all the things I struggle with because of my disability and the hardships of life. But, believe it or not, this old, broken body is full of joy and contentment. And it takes, pardon my French, a hell of a lot more faith to get here than to be healed.

So the question is, if I don't want to be confined to a disabled label, then how do people describe me. Well, I'll tell you, I'm not someone who is confined to a wheelchair. My name is not *disability.* And for all the uneducated, cerebral palsy is a condition and not a disease. I am a *person* who needs a little bit of help along the way, no different from you, no different from society, no different from a church who is trying to find the heart of God. So stop defining me by the term *disabled* and just accept that I am one of you. My weakness is just more evident than the next person's.

Yes, my life is still difficult. I still have many challenges day to day. From this day forward, based on the last ten years, I can accurately assume that the rest of my life will be in pain. Oftentimes it gets scary for me to live on my own. Knowing that I could fall or have a seizure and not be found for hours or even days at a time makes me nervous.

I can't put away my disability and pretend that everything is great like so many people do. I wonder what would happen if people on a daily basis started to pull out their hidden afflictions, weaknesses, failures, and disappointments. To make things more interesting, let's take those afflictions, weaknesses, failures, and disappointments and compare them with the definition of a disability. This would be an exercise that many would decline. Why? Because of their fears. The truth is they would not want to live with the stereotypes that would be forever placed on them. They would be afraid of being excommunicated by society and the local community. They would be afraid of hearing the church tell them that they are no longer good enough to be used by God. This will never happen because people are afraid of being in the situation that I was in, afraid of being exposed to rejection, abuse, and marked as unworthy. They are confined to their fears of being transparent and vulnerable. They know that society will try desperately to lock them away.

My issue with the disabled label is that it is absolute. It seems that people who understand this term don't understand the biology term *metamorphosis*. Someone with a birth defect can still grow and learn. The disabled label doesn't afford the flexibility for someone to evolve. There is life within this cocoon of a body I live in. I have encountered many people who do not have the patience for me to demonstrate this fact. They expect me to remain the same creature that crawled around. They don't realize that within this cocoon, I am gaining the strength to one day fly.

Because of this label, people expect me to continue to be Chris the Caterpillar. There is an expectation on me to remain an individual who gets around on the earth by crawling his way through life. I am no longer Chris the Caterpillar. I am Christopher the Butterfly. Christopher the Butterfly can fly above his circumstances. He is a beautiful symbol of God's mercy, grace, and power. I have experienced a spiritual and personal breakthrough. I will one day mount up on wings like an eagle.

—————⟫•◇•⟪—————

Your Moment with America's Unconfined Life Coach, Motivational Speaker, Author, and Confidence Builder:

People fail to embrace who they truly are because of their fear of being rejected and the fear of being in the middle of a society that is not prepared to take them in. Our inability to have transparent and meaningful relationships is because of our fear of being rejected by society.

Are you whole as you are?
What will it take for you to be spiritually or emotionally content?
Meanwhile, are you living your life?

CHAPTER 24

The Hard Road to Freedom

The Voice of Experience: Chris

I have found a group of people who are more discontent with their lives than I ever was. It's a group called Christian singles. There is actually a Web site called christiansingles.net that hosts thousands of singles who are discontent with their lives because they put marriage and kids ahead of anything else. They believe that until they are married with kids, their life is meaningless. According to them, the first act of being a real Christian is to have a family. Where did this come from? The truth is it came from the church. This is what the church makes young singles believe. Until they are married, they are not valued.

I am so sick of the people that constantly come up to me and say, "I am praying for your wife. I am praying that you get married soon. I am praying for that special one. I know God has a special girl set aside for you. I know she is waiting for you," so on and so on. Well, first of all, I don't want a girl that is waiting for me when she should be out there doing something more with her life. Second, I now hold no one responsible for me feeling complete with my life. I am complete because of God and who I know He created me to be. Furthermore, I don't want the pressure of feeling I am the one that completes someone else's life. Finally, I wonder if those who are praying for me to have a wife are those who would not be happy and full of joy without their spouse. I wonder if their spouse has become their identity. I wonder if God even hears their prayers because in their prayers they are doubting that a person can be whole without a spouse and kids. I wonder if, by praying for me, they are revealing to God their lack of trust and faith.

My sexuality and work in ministry remained a big issue for me. To make matters worse, I met Tim, who was very involved in my life and ministry. Tim was the first person that I ever verbalized my sexual struggles to other than a counselor. I felt like he had accepted me the way that I was and was trying to encourage me to hang in there and do the godly thing.

Over the years, Tim and I became so comfortable with each other that we joked around and shared thoughts that we would never share with another person. About midway into our friendship, he started to make my struggles very difficult. First, it began with sexual jokes then it moved towards inappropriate physical contact. Our wrestling and playing around was starting to feel less than two men challenging each other's manhood and more like sexual contact.

My counseling and the past has come up many times in our relationship. He even agreed and initiated the idea of keeping me accountable to staying on the right track. Yet he still initiated these inappropriate wrestling matches. Let's give him the benefit of the doubt and say that I took things the wrong way. That would be OK except for one thing: he knew. He knew about my past; he knew about things that I struggled with. He knew about the thoughts I was having and the emotions that I was feeling. By the way he was playing around with me he had to know what he was doing.

Tim even suggested that I get back into counseling. I took his suggestion. When the counselor asked me what brought me here, just as I have done with all the other counselors, I explained everything that happened to me up until that very day. He said to me, "You know who you are, and the truth is you have come to terms with that. Unlike many men, you have put boundaries around your life that prevent other people from getting hurt. I will continue to work with you, but it's Tim who really, truly needs counseling."

I believe there is a reason why my counselor suggested that for Tim. You see, I told him of the times when Tim would begin to feel convicted because he was a father, husband, and deacon of his church. Therefore, he would begin to express anger towards me and challenge me to get my life "right." He would never admit to his inappropriate behavior in these situations. This started to bother me heavily. In the middle of going back and forth, there was a woman that he included in his inappropriate jokes. She too saw him initiate inappropriate physical behavior. But he continued to deny that this was an issue for him just as it was for me. He just continued to deny his struggles and blamed me for the inappropriateness when he felt convicted by it. It finally came to a point that he understood that he was making my struggles even more difficult; therefore, the relationship ended altogether. He never once really admitted to the truth.

Tim cannot deal with his reality because he doesn't want someone to doubt his relationship with Christ. Tim does not want to deal with the stigma that the church puts on a person that has a same sex attraction. So he has built a marriage and kids around him, hoping that the Christian world can't see through all of that and therefore won't reject him. What happens when Tim is weak and vulnerable and not getting all that he needs out of that marriage? What does he run to when he and his wife are in an argument and he is looking for something to escape from the reality of the situation?

These are questions that I must keep in the back of my head. I know of many people who hide their preferences and temptations, marry someone, have kids; and then ten years later, they leave their family for someone of the same sex. They cannot deal with not being true to themselves and dealing with the feelings they have suppressed for so long. So they end up ruining their spouse's perception of a healthy marriage as well as their children's. This is one of the reasons why I personally feel that I should never get married.

The church is so bound and determined to protect God's institution of marriage. Yet they have done more damage to marriages than the same sex movement would ever do. Forcing a person to live in the closet opens them up to more sin than ever before. Hiding this reality from the church forces people to live a second life. I know this first hand.

I have been in my new home now for at least two and a half years. My home was a beautiful four-bedroom ranch on one acre of land. I enjoyed so many summer nights and Saturday evenings on my front porch. There was just one problem—I could not go any further than the mailbox on my own. I was confined in my own home. The city of Acworth, Georgia, was a rural place with no sidewalks. I could not get any place without having someone drive me. Most of my friends were now married with children and spent most of their time doing family activities. So needless to say, I spent a lot of days and nights alone. These four walls started to feel like the environment I thought I would be getting away from when I moved to Georgia. The fact that the city of Acworth, Georgia is not wheelchair friendly continues to make life especially difficult. Due to the combination of all of this, I found myself confined to my home on most weekends. There are times that the weekends turned into four or five days if my personal assistant needed time off for any reason.

These long, lonely days are many times accompanied by many seizures and a time of fatigue and weakness. Sometimes, it gets so hard to take care of myself. As I said earlier in this memoir a person with disabilities still has the longing for companionship and intimacy. This fact converted the home I lived in into a lonely, dark closet. I looked for ways that I could bring some light into the days of loneliness.

Most of the time, I couldn't call or reach out to anyone due to their busy family schedules, the time of night or their work commitments. One night on the computer I ran across a website advertising local escorts. Unfortunately, I developed a relationship with four escorts in the area. Sex was never part of our relationships. I was one of many clients who just wanted companionship and intimacy. I knew them personally. We talked about what they wanted to do with their lives, why they were in this profession and many other topics. Because our relationship wasn't sexual, many times they came over after a seizure. When they were not able to come physically visit me they became my mobile companions. This is the one thing in my life that I am ashamed of. Though I know what actually went on behind those closed and lonely doors, I feel ashamed that I needed to hire someone for companionship.

The Voice of Understanding: Christopher

A year and a half later, four days after my thirty-ninth birthday, a difficult yet freeing chapter of my life began. Looking back on it, I realize these things needed to take place in order to truly live an unconfined life. Something I learned about being independent and disabled is after several days of cooking, cleaning, and taking care of oneself, your body gets fatigued. Mentally, you are not as alert as you should be.

On October 24, 2012, while cooking, a task that I have been doing for myself for the last seventeen years, a towel found its way into the gas burner. My attempt to put out the fire resulted in falling and being sandwiched in between the stove and my wheelchair. By the time I was able to regain understanding of my surroundings, the kitchen was completely on fire. I remember thinking to myself: *I've got to get the hell out of here, NOW!*

I started crawling toward the front door. On my way out, I grabbed my man-bag, laptop, and keys that were sitting on the table by the front door. Now, on a normal day, I am not quick on my feet. Under these conditions, I certainly wasn't thinking to my full capacity. However, the idea popped into my head to hit the remote on my key chain, which caused my car alarm to go off. The alarm grabbed my neighbors attention and caused him to look up and see smoke coming from my house. By the time I got the door open, my neighbor was running full speed up the front porch. He grabbed me and carried me across the street.

There in my neighbor's front yard, I sat and watched everything I've owned burn in the fire. Any symbol of what I have accomplished over the last thirty-nine years was being destroyed right before my very eyes. I was numb with the thought of starting over. Where would I get the energy to rebuild my middle-class life? It takes the same amount of effort for a man with a severe disability in the United States to establish a middle-class lifestyle as it would for a perfectly able man to become a self-made millionaire.

Thank God for the many friends who did so much to help me in the beginning of my challenges. I don't know what I would have done without their friendship. Unfortunately, that was just the beginning of the challenges that many friendships did not endure.

While dealing with the insurance claim, I decided that I needed to explore different areas in Atlanta that may be wheelchair friendly. I found the most accessible places for me were areas called Midtown and Atlantic Station. I loved the accessibility and convenience both locations offered a person who depends on a wheelchair for mobility. However, Midtown was a predominately gay area. Whereas just across the interstate was Atlantic Station, a more conservative area. I worked hard with my real estate agent to try to find a condo in the Atlantic Station area. However, the place I immediately fell in love with was right in the middle of Midtown. I had an issue with this not because of my feelings toward people with different sexual preferences, but I knew my feelings and my desires would come to surface. I knew that I would be able to truly be myself and that I would fit very well in this community. I also knew that a lot of my friends and family would not approve of this. They would question why I moved into this community. Living here would not be a great thing for my career after spending thirteen years speaking to predominantly Christian organizations. Yet the price was right, so I decided that this was the best place for me.

Within a couple of months of being in this environment, I knew I could no longer ignore the reality I tried to hide for most of my life. The fact was I could continue to go to all the counseling and tell myself over and over it wasn't true. Like it or not, I am attracted to the same sex. Same sex attraction is not purely a physical feeling like most people think. The truth is I feel, along with many others, that we can have a stronger connection with a member of the same sex more than we can with a member from the opposite sex. The connection I have experienced with a man is the same connection we all need to have a strong relationship with someone intimately. The thought of what that meant to my friendships and career overwhelmed me. I became very depressed and did not know how to deal with the reality of my situation. For a while, I thought that the best thing I could do was to give up. For the second time in my life, in thirty-nine years of a hard life, I thought suicide was the answer twice in a six-month period.

Those six months were the hardest times of my life. While being evaluated for the first attempt, a guy who I considered to be one of my closest friends invaded my privacy by going through my cell phone and reading text messages and emails dating back over a two-year time frame. He discovered conversations I have had with the escorts I have hired in the past and other males I have built mobile relationships with through mobile apps. Unfortunately, he did not confront me and allow me to deal with this sensitive reality in my own time. Instead he decided to share this information with three other friends. These friends of mine felt that the Christian thing to do was to make sure everyone knew of my private life. They did not care that I needed more time after just trying to end my life a few weeks ago. They demanded a "Come to Jesus" meeting. At that meeting and over the course of the next couple of weeks, they strong-armed me into coming out and telling all my friends, supporters, and past clients of my "sinful lifestyle." I asked them to give me more time because I was already in the process of writing this memoir in which I had every intention of sharing my story, in my time and in my own way. However, they did not extend to me that right. They were convinced that this needed to happen now and if I didn't do so they would. They truly believed that this was the correct Biblical course of action.

It takes people a lifetime to come to the realization of who they really are, if they ever do. Most don't. What most people may look over when reading this book is it took me twenty years to come to grips with my sexuality. It wasn't just a decision that I haphazardly made. Then some want to know why it took me so long? Why did I hide my sexuality for so long? There were many times I wanted to tell someone or have the freedom to go on a date. I wasn't hiding, I was trying to come to grips with it. It doesn't matter if a person knows of their sexuality at an early age or later in life, it takes time to come to term with being attracted to the same sex. Anyone in their right mind would struggle with subjecting themselves to the ridicule they would have to face for being gay in this country. There is a segment of this country that still looks down upon black people. A larger segment of the country devalue me because I am disabled. It is also very clear how people feel about people who are gay. Of course I would think twice every time I wanted to "come out." Something would be wrong with me mentally if I didn't see how hard it would be. Who can't see how this would be difficult for me?

I understand that some people won't "buy it." They feel like they had a right to know. There is something I need to say to those people

and the rest of the world, "It is not about you! It is not about your
personal or religious beliefs. It is not about your sexual preferences
or what you feel comfortable with. My life is about me and the
things I believe my God is telling me. I am sorry if you thought "our
relationship" was all about you.

Of course, I got the rude e-mails and phone calls. Now everybody's
good Christian friend was a "no-good fag and a worthless nigger."
Someone told me that I would be better off dead. That way, I would
not shame the Christian faith. Many letters came in the mail. One
of them told me I needed to repent. But it came from the same
person who said President Obama was the Antichrist. Now the
right thing to do is treat me as someone who does not know the
Lord. I did not know the best way to treat a non-Christian was to
put their livelihood in jeopardy, make them feel like crap for not
having the same sexual desires as the next person, and break off all
communication with them. That kind of treatment will make people
run to the church, right?

All of my fears and concerns were correct. Friends who I stood by
for many years turned their backs on me. I walked with these friends
of mine through divorces, affairs, and many other life challenges. I
was the person that many of their children called when they were
about to do something stupid. I went with them to their sexual
addiction groups. I was the one that got the late phone calls from
people about to take their own lives. My ten-year commitment to
these friendships was no longer valuable to them.

Over the next couple of months things got seemingly worse.
Because I was no longer receiving speaking engagements and a lot
of my supporters stopped contributing, I got behind on my financial
responsibilities. The phone calls, the threats of repossession, hate mail
and the feeling of being excommunicated from friends and family
were overwhelming. At the same time I realized over the years another
friend of mine was taking advantage of me while I was unconscious
and disoriented from a seizure. This reality devastated me and yielded

my second suicide attempt. Fortunately, once again my attempt was unsuccessful but the second attempt put the nail in the coffin. Everyone who did not read the memo now knew of my sexuality.

One thing I have learned about spirituality is there is an element of faith and brainwashing in it no matter the person's religious beliefs. There are things people just believe without opposing it. That is faith. The truth is the truth; a person should not kill another person. Then there are things we believe because of a good argument. Drinking is wrong. That line of reasoning can be right for someone who has have bad experiences with drinking. It is ok for them to be brainwashed to believe this. Many can see how their religion supports this. The argument many times produces great ideals and principles that work in the life of the individual; therefore, they should adopt those ideals and principles. It would be healthy for that person. The problem comes in when those brainwashed ideals and principles becomes Jesus' commandments for everyone. We have to find and understand the line between faith and healthy brainwashing. Good ideals and principles are not necessarily God's commandments. Anything that is not based on absolute truth requires the individual to allow themselves to be brainwashed to the ideal or principal. A lot of people are brainwashed to believe a person can't be gay and Christian. That is not truth. God never said you must be heterosexual to be a Christian.

A very good friend of mine was concerned, not so much about my sexuality as much as he was concerned with labeling myself as "gay" or "homosexual." He said I am not *that* type of person. I knew his heart and where he was coming from. The truth is there are many people who adopt stereotypes as truths. There is no doubt about it. There is a segment of the gay population that is promiscuous, perverted or even flamboyant. To be fair, the heterosexual population also has members in it that represent those characteristics as well. I agree there are ignorant people out there who have used this reality to label the whole homosexual population. Some people have failed to realize that they work with, worship with and have homosexual and bisexual people in their families. Let's be realistic. There are gay doctors, lawyers, teachers, and yes, pastors. They are good people with hearts, minds and souls.

My life would be a lot easier if I was white, perfectly able and heterosexual. I will admit that having the same sex attraction is not an easy road to be on as an American, disabled man or a Christian. The church's ideals and principles on the subject, maybe healthy somehow for some Christians to be brainwashed into believing. However, "You can't be gay and Christian," is not what the Bible tells me. For me to live an unconfined spiritual life I can't mix-up man's biased opinions with God's truth. I am able to separate church from God. As a disabled man I can tell you that is the most important ability to have.

Your Moment with America's Unconfined Life Coach, Motivational Speaker, Author, and Confidence Builder:

There is a song I used to listen to. The main lyrics of this song says "What's done in the dark, will come to the light." This truth can be haunting or liberating. If you squint your eyes and fall back into a corner it is haunting. But if you open your eyes, stand strong and live up to the things that once confined you, you will then be liberated.

What is your darkness?
What needs to be brought to the light?
Are there coping methods in your life you need to get rid of?

CHAPTER 25

Truth vs. Biased Opinion

The Voice of Understanding: Christopher

The things we, Christians, label as blessings and curses are sometimes crazy, if not sadistic. For example, no one questions my disability. Even though there were so many things that went wrong in the delivery room that night. In the Bible, there are many verses that suggest that a disability is the result of sin. Yet, I have met thousands of people and been to hundreds of churches that totally accepted my disability as God's plan for my life. However, my sexuality makes them uncomfortable so it must be a sin. I feel that most of the people that were in my life was ok with me being different from them as long as our differences inspired them and required me to suffer for "Christ." I was out of their lives the minute our differences meant that they would have to be uncomfortable and allow me to find some happiness in my life. Now, in so many words those same people are saying, "We should not be uncomfortable so let's use the Bible to segregate ourselves from him." Like people did with women, blacks and disabled people in the past.

Now lets be real. There are straight people who went through the same dysfunctional scenarios I did or worse. There are gay people who had a great upbringing. I cannot say that anything in my past made me attracted to the same sex. Psychologist, ministers and many bias people have their explanations for same sex attraction. Some of the clinical reasons are: people chose to be gay, they are seduced or tricked into identifying themselves as gay, people are gay because of their parents, they are gay because of their biology, they are gay because of physical brain differences, it is because of the older brother effects; and finally the one I personally believe in, we don't know. The group that has the hardest time with the "we don't know," explanation are the ones that believes that God uniquely made everyone and has a plan for their lives. There are about 18 million gay people in the US alone. The church tells them all to "go away." Sometimes we soften the message and add, "Until you are straight or repent of your sexual sin." I am not ashamed of the Gospel but I am ashamed of the church.

If a person's sexuality was a huge issue that God had, I believe He would have used Jesus and the New Testament to deal with it boldly and clearly. God would have dealt with it and called it out the way He did with adultery, covertness, hypocrisy, taking care of the poor, and judging other people. We act as if we got all of the above right, and now it's time to find other things Jesus might or should have a problem with. To be honest, the church spends more time and effort on this issue than God does. This is why many people still ask me how do I reconcile the Bible with my sexuality. (They don't ask me, how am I dealing with the fact that my fears of being judged and condemn by them, made me want to take my life.) They ask for my interpretation of several verses that they believe to classify same sex relationships as sin. Some have assumed that I don't know what these verses are or their meaning. As a Christian and a gay man I have spent many, many days and nights researching the scriptures that are commonly used to argue the point that same sex relationships are sinful. Those scriptures are: Leviticus 18:21-22, 19:19, 19:28; Galatians 3:22; Genesis 19:5; I Corinthians 6:9-10; Ezekial 16:49; I Timothy 9:10; and Romans 1:26.

I have read hundreds of online articles on this issue, listened to sermons and heard numerous debates on the pros and cons of same sex relationships. I have reminisced on all the things that I have learned in church over the years. Also, through the Gaychristiannetwork.org I have introduced myself to the gay Christian world. And finally, I have researched those nine verses back to their original language in order to get the true biblical interpretation of the scriptures.

Yes, I did my research to help me understand God's plan for my own life. I also did this because the gay community is worth the time needed to research the scriptures. I hope my Christian brothers, sisters and friends would agree with me and invest themselves, spirits, minds and hearts to make sure that these scriptures do indeed restrict gay people from their lives, churches and heaven. With that said I present to you my research on five of the nine verses that are quoted most often.

Leviticus 18:22, 20:13 Deuteronomy 23:17-18

"Thou shalt not lie with mankind, as with womankind: it is abomination." - Leviticus 18:22

"If a man also lie with mankind, as he lieth with a woman, both of them have committed an abomination: they shall surely be put to death; their blood shall be upon them." – Leviticus 20:13

"There shall be no whore of the daughters of Israel, nor a sodomite of the sons of Israel. Thou shalt not bring the hire of a whore, or the price of a dog, into the house of the Lord thy God for any vow: for even both these are abomination unto the Lord thy God." - Deuteronomy 23:17-18

Before we use Deuteronomy and Leviticus to tag people as an abomination, we should know the meaning of the word. Let's be sure we are not condemning ourselves. Abomination comes from the Hebrew word "toebah" meaning something morally revolting or loathing of something connected with idolatry. There are many things the author of these books considered to be an abomination, like: touching or eating anything with "impurity" (catfish, lobster, shrimp, oysters, clams, mussels etc.), customs associated with the worship of anything other-than-God, idols, any action a person does that is not done in the name of God, cheating, atheists, one that departs from God, those that lie, people who shed innocent blood, those that cause distress, evil, trouble or wrong toward others, lying about another person, people that cause trouble in a community, cheating in business or exchanges of money, inauthentic sacrifice and repentance, doing things for yourself and not God, pride, passing sentence or judgment on an innocent man or letting an evil man go free, cheating others in property or matters of goods, people that turn from hearing God's Word, the prayers of an evil person, sacrificed meat eaten on the third day instead of being burned, men having sex with men, any superstitious relic, an imperfect animal offering, anyone who visits tarot card or palm readers or who reads horoscopes, wearing clothes of the opposite sex, bringing money earned from prostitution from selling yourself into your home, remarrying a former spouse, cheating people, making images or idols, having the idols of certain gods in your possession, prayers not offered in faith, human sacrifices, robbery, murder, adultery, oppression of others that are poor or vulnerable, violence, breaking promises, lending money with interest, having sex with a menstruating woman, injustice, worship of anti-Christ, incest, and things done to gain popularity with others.

Also, the combination of different kinds of anything was not allowed, or vile to a Jew like: mixing seeds in fields, interbreeding animals, mixing fabrics in clothing and letting disabled people come to the holy place. Is doing something detestable or abominable sinful and is not kingdom worthy? "Toevah" is the Hebrew word. It means ritually unclean and is often used in association with idolatry. The forbidden, or detestable things were generally used in idol worship. These actions were happening while worshiping in the temples.

There are many things in these books that are so bad that they are punishable by death: denying God and saying He does not exist, getting too close to the Tabernacle when you were not supposed to be there, not observing the Sabbath, disobeying one's parents, cursing or hitting one's parents, sexual intercourse with a woman that has her menstrual cycle, losing your virginity outside "marriage," adultery, being a false prophet, male homosexual sex, witchcraft, worshiping other gods, using God's name in vain, bestiality, rape, a woman who does not cry out when being raped, witchcraft, murder, and kidnapping. If we are going to be legalistic with the Word, then let's do that. Who is not guilty of abominations, of detestable behavior, of actions worth the penalty of death in the Old and New Testaments? If we still want to abide by laws given to Jews in the Books of the Law, then we have to abide by all of them. That means we all should be killed along with people who are gay.

Lets put away our denominational stances, doctrinal beliefs, cultural and religious biases; this is really about the translation of words. In Deuteronomy they translated the word "whore" to "temple prostitute," "sodomite," "shrine prostitute." They appear in Hebrew as "qadesh," meaning a temple male prostitute and "qedeshah" meaning a female prostitute. Yet, they often have been translated as "homosexual" and "sodomite." The word is qadesh, prostitute. They were indeed having gay sex, but they were doing it in the framework of idol worship here. That is the problem in these verses; prostitution and idol worshipping.

I Corinthians 6:9-11, I Timothy 1:9-11

I Corinthians and I Timothy are the two most difficult scriptures to interpret when researching what the Bible says about homosexuality. When analyzing verses, it is important to examine context, original language and culture. Not so easy to do here though. The two Greek words used in I Corinthians and I Timothy are "arsenokoitai" and "malakoi," which were originated from Paul.

> "Neither the sexually immoral nor idolaters nor adulterers nor male prostitutes ("malakoi/malakos") nor homosexual offenders ("arsenokoitai") nor thieves nor the greedy nor drunkards nor slanderers nor swindlers will inherit the kingdom of God. And that is what some of you were. But you were washed, you were sanctified, you were justified in the name of the Lord Jesus Christ and by the Spirit of our God." - I Corinthians 6:9-11

In I Corinthians 6:9-11 "malakoi/malakos" means: of uncertain affinity, soft, that is fine clothing, figuratively a catamite, effeminate. I remind you to put away your denominational stances, doctrinal beliefs, cultural and religious biases; this is really about the translation of words. "Malakoi" is translated in modern Bibles as: effeminate in NASB, men who practice homosexuality in ESV, male prostitute in NIV, pervert in CEV, and homosexual in NKJV.

It was only in the last fifty years or so the word "homosexual," appeared in the Bible. In the 1960's to 1970's there was a shift in the words in the Bible. The word "malakoi" started its drift from "male prostitute" to "homosexual." But, God is the same yesterday, today and tomorrow. Think about what was going on during that time. The world was changing fast and people were uncomfortable with it. Could it be that cultural bias crept into the Word of God to place man's discomfort and disgust on a group of people they personally did not like, feared or even hated? It wouldn't be the first time in bible history.

"We also know that the law is made not for the righteous but for lawbreakers and rebels, the ungodly and sinful, the unholy and irreligious; for those who kill their fathers or mothers, for murderers, for adulterers and perverts ("arsenokoitai"), for slave traders and liars and perjurers—and for whatever else is contrary to the sound doctrine that conforms to the glorious gospel of the blessed God, which he entrusted to me." - I Timothy 1:9-11

How will you do when I Timothy is applied to your life? He tells us to have no god before Him nor to serve any idols. Also, He tells us not to blaspheme Him and to honor His day. He told us to honor our parents and not kill. He said not to commit adultery or steal. He told us not to lie. The truth is, we all do actions against the Law and against the gospel of God. And by the time we are out of one sin we are in another! We all break His commandments.

ROMANS 1:26-28

"For this cause God gave them up unto vile affections: for even their women did change the natural use into that which is against nature: And likewise also the men, leaving the natural use of the woman, burned in their lust one toward another; men with men working that which is unseemly, and receiving in themselves that recompence of their error which was meet. And even as they did not like to retain God in their knowledge, God gave them over to a reprobate mind, to do those things which are not convenient;" - Romans 1:26-28

What is going on here? The people had a conversion experience. Then they started to worship unnatural things and the gods of the State again. They were involved in idol worship and some of it had sexual expressions. They also participated in culturally acceptable practices to a Roman, but, not to a Jewish Christian. They had abandoned the truth of God and went back to their old gods of nature and created things. Because of this, God gave them over to their own desires. What is the "this?" They had turned from God, having known Him, and returned to their idolatrous worship. They had returned to worshiping creatures, nature, people and not

God. The "this" is a turning from God, who they once knew, and returning to idols.

What kinds of actions were they doing once they turned back to their old ways? The Bible says women had exchanged the natural use of their body for an unnatural use. Read the verse. It does not say women were having sex with women. It could have been sex with other women, sex during menstruation, oral sex or sex with an uncircumcised man. All of these behaviors were "unnatural" to a Jewish Christian.

Now let's look at the words and see if just the actions of men having sex with men, or women having sex with women is enough to garner God's eternal damnation. Different versions of the Bible will translate "shameful lusts" as "vile affections." "Vile" comes from the Greek word "atimai" which means infamy, indignity, dishonor, reproach and shame.

In Matthew 12 and in Mark 3 the only deed that produces absolute cutting off from God is to eternally refuse the Holy Spirit. These new Gentile converts knew God, knew the Spirit and went back to the old patterns of worship and behavior. That was the ultimate "sin" according to Paul. Can unnatural use of a body be the thing that cuts you off from God eternally? Original language is again the key.

"Natural use" is "phusikos chrēsis," an instinctive use and in this case, an instinctive sexual use. Further, it means what is consistent, expected, ordinary and usual. When someone behaves in a "natural" way, they are being consistent with what you, or in this case, the writer, would expect. Does that mean behaving in "unnatural" way is then wrong, immoral or sinful? "Against nature" is "para phusis" or contrary to the usual, natural, expected way. Men with long hair in the times of Paul were not only "unnatural" / "para phusis," but vile/" atimia " as well.

In Romans 11:24, it says "After all, if you were cut out of an olive tree that is wild by nature, and contrary to nature (para phusis) were grafted into a cultivated olive tree, how much more readily will these, the natural branches, be grafted into their own olive tree!" Paul is talking about God's new way of doing things; He chosen to attach the Gentiles into the same family as the Jews. This was very unexpected, very unnatural, very out of the usual. If God can be "para phusis" and not be sinful, surely other things can be "para phusis" and not be sinful.

In Romans 1:27 and 28 the same word "natural" is used again. To the Jew, there were approved intentions in sex. It was between a man and a woman and it was normal coitus. Not so in the Roman culture. There was an order of hierarchy within sexual activities of adult Roman citizens. They could have penetrative sex with women, male and female slaves or non-citizens and with youth. The only unacceptable sex within that society was male sex between citizens of equal social class. That was the traditions of that time and that place. The Gentile converts had reverted back to their old social norms. It is a wholesomeness issue.

How do we know that the sexual acts were not seen as sin? Paul had already used words for sin. In verse 18, he used "godlessness and wickedness" when describing people who "suppressed the truth." Those words are "asebia" and "adikia" which both mean something behaviorally incorrect, sin.

God did not say people that are involved in same sex relationships are going to hell. This was about people that once knew Him and had now turned from Him. The audience of Paul's letter were relying on cultural dislikes. They were splitting the church over their rules, not God's rules. We are doing the same thing today; not over what is pure and impure, but over heterosexual and homosexual.

We don't get to say long hair is okay and unnatural use of a body is not okay. We may be more comfortable with people with long hair than gay people, but that becomes a cultural thing and cannot be somehow made into an action equivalent of "blaspheming the Holy Spirit" or make it into a "damned to hell" sentencing. No matter how much we dislike a behavior according to our own valuations, we do not get to change the words to mean what we want them to say. And most importantly we do not get to settle on what we believe the verses to say without intense study. If we are calling ourselves believers and followers, we have to try to view things through God's eyes, not our own. Putting our cultural slants, societal prejudices and dislikes on a group is quite human, but to label that judgment as if it is God's scales of justice is going beyond the scale of Scripture.

While studying these verses I received a call from the Pastor of the church that I am currently a member of. He told me that a young man who recently came out took his life because of the pressure of being attracted to the same sex. This hit close to home because in the last six months I have been very close to taking the same course of action. In that moment, one thing echoed in my head, that was the voice of a supposed friend of mine saying, "You will glorify God more by killing yourself than coming out and admitting to your sexuality." At first I didn't know how to respond to that, but now after thinking about this kids death I can say, "That is a lie straight from Hell! Not only that but the individual who said this to me is further away from God than he thinks I am."

As you can tell my research on these scriptures are quite lengthy and in detail. Going into the other four scriptures would make this a very long chapter. However, I encourage you to go back and do your own research on all nine scriptures. My only caveat is that you make sure you use a Strong's concordance from 1880 before the biased opinions of others began to infiltrate the Word of God.

Now I know a lot of people will allow my research of the scripture to go in one ear and out the other. They will choose not to research the scripture for themselves and search for the truth. Many Christians would rather remain ignorant than put aside their biased opinion. For those people who failed to do their own research and just take the word for face value knowing that it has been interpreted time and time again over many years, I want to challenge you to the truth. Personal biases are not of God. I hope we can move beyond them. As uncomfortable as we may feel with any group of "others," personal biases are not love. They are not reflective of Jesus.

If you chose not to put aside your biased opinions and research the scripture then the truth is for you, same sex relationships are not about the Bible or Christ. Instead this issue is about the things you personally are not comfortable with. Because you are not comfortable with people in same sex relationships you have adopted the traditional mindsets and opinions that have led this country down the road of bigotry, racism and segregation for so many years. I believe the saying is, "Lets call a spade a spade." Many who are uncomfortable with same sex behavior are mimicking the same racial behavior minorities had to deal with in our nation's past. This approach is why Sunday morning remains to be the most segregated time of the week in the U.S. Unfortunately, many churches have always been and continue to be the leaders in segregation.

People need to know that in spite of what they believe I am still madly in love with God and continue to have faith in Jesus Christ. Several individuals assume that because of my sexuality I am walking away from my faith. The truth is I feel more drawn to Him now than ever before. I think it is because of the fact that my relationship with Him is no longer confined to my relationship with other believers. Many have walked away allowing me to redefine what a relationship in Christ looks like. Now I understand what unconditional love is and how rare it truly is. Now knowing what unconditional love really looks like, my faith and dedication to Him has been strengthened.

I know so many people are expecting me to say, "I am now unworthy to be called a child of God." I never was worthy of being a child of God. And if you think you being heterosexual makes you more worthy than I am then Satan has you right where he wants you. That is eating out of his hands.

As a persecuted Christian, I understand grace, mercy and justice. Yes persecuted; I have been discounted, invalidated and told that I am an oxymoron, and yet, I still stand in Him. And I have been rejected and scorned by the gay community at large for being a traitor and for siding with the enemy, the church, and the very group that reviles their community, yet I am remaining steadfast. Unless you have been in my position personally to witness it, you cannot evaluate my heart. Even when the bulk of the church will not acknowledge my position, I will maintain it.

Your Moment with America's Unconfined Life Coach, Motivational Speaker, Author, and Confidence Builder:

We are too quick to pass judgment and label people based on our biased opinions as Christians. I don't believe personally that people are fallen from the ministry as much as they are fallen from the pedestal we have put them on.

Is God wise enough to understand that every man has fallen short and is in need of mercy and grace regardless of their beliefs and occupation?
Is God sovereign enough to use our pitfalls and failures to glorify and magnify His name?
Shouldn't we hold off and wait around long enough for God to show us who He is before we judge, condemn, and sentence a man?

CHAPTER 26

Past, Present & Future

The Voice of Understanding: Christopher

Let me remind you, of something I shared with you in Chapter 12, because you might see the significance of it all. A person who is allowing their surroundings to be boundaries around their potential is living a confined life. Individuals are the core of their atmosphere. Their atmosphere is made up of layers that many times need to be carved away to find their true potential. Our family's perspective on life is the first and closest layer around our core. The collective mentality of the environment around us is the next layer. Then we have the stereotypes that society places on us because of our immediate environment. These layers do not destroy one's potential; they simply hide them. The individual has the responsibility to pull back the layers and expose his or her true potential.

Peeling an apple is not about reaching the core as much as it is about exposing the core. The core of an apple is the only thing that is not eaten up. The person who is not eaten up by life is the one that focuses on his potential rather than his surroundings. I knew there was something in me that had to find a way out. I had to show it to the rest of the world. I believed when the layers of my hard life are peeled back, something great would be discovered.

After everything I've been through in the past three to fours years, it's hard to believe I'm here. I really thought that I would never return to a state of joy again. Deep down inside, for so many years, I felt guilty for loving who I am. I am a black disabled gay Christian. Society frowns upon the things that plays a major role in who I am. Knowing this made me want to give-up. That is no longer the case. I am moving forward with a sense of peace in my heart. Even though I lost my home in a fire, I've been forced to "come out" about my sexuality, had to re-build my career and lost friends I really love; the big "Kool-aid smile" remains on my face. I love my life now more than ever before. I feel free to love who I am and what I have become over the years.

I remember when this song came out: "You don't know the cost of my alabaster box." An alabaster box is a box that is carved out of a very expensive stone. Many people keep valuable things in this box. There was a lady in the Bible who had one of these very same boxes, and she kept very rare and expensive perfume and oil in it. This lady meets Jesus, and she takes her alabaster box and pours the very rare and expensive perfume over Jesus, but what most people don't know is this is a lady that God has called out of prostitution. God tells her early on in the scripture, "Go and sin no more," and now she is taking the very box and the very oil that she probably bought with her prostitution money, money that she no longer had and would not be able to replace, because God called her out of her profession. She used the last of this perfume to pour over and bless Jesus.

I think about my life and what things I had to go through to bring Him valuable praise. It is easy to praise Jesus when you haven't gone through something, but it is difficult when your praise requires you to give up something. When you have gone through so much in your life that could have been prevented by God, but for some reason He didn't do it, and you're still praising Him. There is something about giving God your last, not just financially, but your last emotion, your last tear, your last bit of strength. There is something about giving God the very pain that keeps you up at night. That is what I call valuable praise. That is what I believe the song is referring to when it says, "You don't know the cost of my alabaster box." You don't know what I went through. You don't know how hard it is to sit here and praise God after all that I have faced in life.

I believe that it is necessary, as Christians, for us to understand that even though God gives us discernment, we are not given the authority to decide what will be the outcome of people's struggles, temptations, and sin. We must realize that God's sovereignty is not in our hands. We have to be careful not to try to confine Jesus to our beliefs. So to question the joy, contentment, peace, and my calling because of my physical condition, weakness, sin, and sexuality is to question His sovereignty. God's sovereignty is His ability and right to use whatever He views as fit to accomplish His purpose and will. His sovereignty trumps people's understanding, desires, beliefs, weakness, temptations, sins and, yes, even their sexuality.

I hope that this book encourages more Christian people to come out and admit to their sexual preference. I don't want this to happen to make my life any easier. My desire for this to happen is to give people the opportunity to deal with these desires upfront. If a person believes their desires are wrong or unbiblical, then the church ought to provide them a kind and loving environment in which they can get the help they feel they need. If a person believes that this is the way that God wired them and designed them to be, then so be it. The church still has the responsibility of providing a loving and safe environment in which that person can know Christ.

At this point, a lot of people who know me well, including family, may be thinking I am not the person they thought I was. I would agree with that. I am not the person they thought I was. I am stronger than that. I am the person they don't see behind closed doors, who struggles with getting himself dressed in the morning, has multiple seizures in a week, can't drive his own car to go get something to eat, and can't pour himself a glass of milk, yet he chooses to tap into joy and show those around him that they too can live an unconfined life. I am the person who has the courage enough to share his mistakes, struggles, and sins to the world, knowing that he will be judged but hoping that my story would help someone. I am the person that has faced so much abuse and rejection that he has every reason to give up and walk away from religion, yet I haven't given up. Yes, I have walked away from religion but only in my pursuit and desire to follow God. He does not see me as a project to fix but a person to love. I am no longer confined spiritually because I understand that God is bigger than my sexuality, disability and race.

Your Moment with America's Unconfined Life Coach, Motivational Speaker, Author, and Confidence Builder:

PAST

I want to cry right now as I think about the things I went through. So many scary moments. I constantly felt hopeless and worthless. There were times in my life that I felt like all of society had coughed up a loogie and spit it on my face. So many lonely days. I got so sick of being sick. Every time I think I am getting better, something else happens, and I am right back down on the same path again. Also the struggle of a disability doesn't excuse a disabled person from the everyday struggles of life. I still had to face broken relationships, lost relationships, death of loved ones, financial struggles, and growing pains. In all my darkness, there is still an overwhelming feeling inside of me that brings a smile to my face, a sparkle in my eye, and a passion to live the best life while I am here on earth.

Satan tried really hard to ruin my life. He used my situation, my family, the church, and society as tools for his attempts. Even though Christ unlocked my cage, these people were a tool in Satan's hand to keep me confined. I know it wasn't intentional on their part, but Satan knew exactly how to use them. It worked for a while. But in spite of all of that, with God's help, I will live! I will not let those things confine me anymore. When I die, it won't be because I can't stomach life anymore. It will be because I lived life to the fullest.

They say I was born dead, but I came back to life. The truth is, for a long time I was still dead. Like so many, I was waiting for a chance to live. There is a difference between being alive in the body and being alive in the heart, mind, and soul. Just being alive in my body was death. It wasn't until the oxygen reached my heart, mind, and soul and allowed me to exhale, my life began. I was waiting for a chance to exhale all the stuff my life in this body was forcing me to inhale. Most people are living until the day they die, but I was dead, waiting for the opportunity to live. My prayers for the opportunity to smile through my grief are coming true. Though my heart has been broken, I am starting to love. I am letting go of the things that are killing me and reaching out for a lifeline. I am living.

PRESENT

At the age of forty, I am still on my knees, crawling around my home, trying to get from one room to the next, opening my front door only to look up at my guest from the floor. Those guests step over me and around me as if I am a little child in the middle of the floor, in my own home. There is a blessing in that. Many people wake up every day and just go on with their lives, but God has put me in a position that I have to fall to my knees daily. I have to acknowledge Him daily as my strength. I know I can't do anything without Him. He says in His word, "Every knee will bend and every tongue will confess that He is Lord." For some, that won't happen until they find themselves living in eternity, where that will be too late. And some have the opportunity to do it now. I thank God that He has given me no other option.

I often reminisce of the many years I spent dreaming and wondering what my life would be like. "Will I ever have my own home? Will I be able to provide for myself? I want kids. I want to get married." All of those questions and thoughts remained with me daily for many years of my life. And just like any child, I dreamed big dreams. Today I am satisfied. I am satisfied with the broken dreams. I am satisfied with the accomplished goals. And I'm overwhelmed by the things I never would have imagined. My fight for freedom is now accomplished.

I can't believe, after all these years, I have come to a place in my life where I can truly say my disability is a gift from God. I have experienced lots of heartaches, disappointments, and tears. I have made my own mistakes by lying, cheating, and doing whatever I could to survive. Some would say I have every reason to be bitter, complain, and give up. However, I heard someone say one time, "The difference between Peter and Judas was that Peter looked for a reason to follow God, while Judas looked for a reason not to follow God." I am committed to be more like Peter.

I can stand in the grace of God. I can go on because of my experience with Him not because the world hasn't been difficult. Chris found a lifeline in Christ. Through the power of Christ, Chris can be Christopher.

FUTURE

Only time will tell the whole story. But after looking at things in retrospect, I see life a little bit different now. As a disabled man, I know that greatness is not in me, but it flows through me. I can rejoice in the fact that God works great things through the weakest, littlest, and poorest men. God did not change my situation; He changed my heart. Nothing has happened outside of His will. Even my struggles were an avenue for greatness. God—with all His wisdom, knowledge, and strength—chose to form my weakness. I never thought that the answers to all my questions would be that I was created for this.

I am determined not to let my disability dictate how I will live my life. So with that said, I can now say that cerebral palsy did not stop me from jumping out of an airplane! That is right. I went skydiving, and it was amazing. I guess you can call me the disabled James Bond. One week I am escaping a burning building and the next I am jumping out of an airplane.

I learned something while free-falling for forty-five seconds from five thousand feet; gravity and real freedom have something in common. To fully experience gravity and freedom, you must be willing to take a risk. They both give you the opportunity to fly or fall. It doesn't matter your race, gender, size, ability, or disability; gravity and real freedom do not discriminate. It is our decision to live or die. While falling through the air, my instructor and I chose to pull out the parachute just like Harriet Tubman and other slaves chose to utilize the Underground Railroad. If we choose to be free, the only way we can fail is if someone tampers with our right to fly. We all have the ability to live an unconfined life.

When I started the first forty years of my life, I had no control over that. Society has dictated the first four decades of my life. I have lived through their poor decisions and ignorant mind-sets. I think it is fair now that I be the one that makes the decisions for the next forty years of my life. I am looking forward to the second half of my life not being dictated by the disabled label, the dysfunctional society, or the disobedient church. Now I am hoping to fall in love, adopt kids, write my third book, continue to speak all over the world and coach people to live an unconfined life. I would love it if my career would cross path with Oprah Winfrey, Tyler Perry, Ellen DeGeneres, Queen Latifah, T.D. Jakes or Dr. Phil McGrew. Hey, just throwing it out there.

So there you have it: the good, the bad, and the ugly. I've shared with you my successes, failures, victories, and defeats. There has been a lot of joy, laughter, and many not so prideful moments. I've been confined physically, spiritually, professionally, financially, and personally. Now as a life coach, author, speaker and a friend, I want to ask you some questions I've spent most of my career asking people across the country:

What's your wheelchair?

What situation in your life are you allowing to stop you from living an unconfined life?

When does your freedom begin?

Thank you reading my life story. Now that you are at the end, please give my book a review good or bad at Iuniverse.com.
#UnconfinedLife

BIBLIOGRAPHY

Turman, Kathryn, "Working with Victims
of Crime with Disabilities".
www.Mincaba.umm.edu.
April 19, 2001. Web. February 26,2014.

Sobsey, Dick, "The Invincible Victims: An update
originally published in Prosecutors Brief: The California
District Attorneys Associate Director Quarterly
Journal". www.dascentre.edu.ualberta.ca.
August 9, 2002. Web. February 26, 2014.

http://www.ssa.gov/policy/docs/ssb/v67n2/v67n2p73.html

Lou Harris Poll, "Disability Resources". http://www.virtualability.
org/disability-resources/. 2014. Web. February 26, 2014.

Roeher Institute, "People with Disabilities and
Sexual Assault".www.sosiaaliportti.fi.
1995. Web. February 26, 2014